Kenyon College
Gambier, Ohio

Written by Jay Helmer and Zack Rosen
Edited by Kevin Nash

Additional contributions by Adam Burns, Omid Gohari, Christina Koshzow, Chris Mason, Jon Skindzier, Tim Williams, Brianne Conlan, Joey Rahimi, Luke Skurman, and Kimberly Moore

ISBN # 1-59658-071-2
ISSN # 1551-1036
© Copyright 2005 College Prowler
All Rights Reserved
Printed in the U.S.A.
www.collegeprowler.com

Special thanks to Babs Carryer, Andy Hannah, LaunchCyte, Tim O'Brien, Bob Sehlinger, Thomas Emerson, Andrew Skurman, Barbara Skurman, Bert Mann, Dave Lehman, Daniel Fayock, Chris Babyak,The Donald H. Jones Center for Entrepreneurship, Terry Slease, Jerry McGinnis, Bill Ecenberger, Idie McGinty, Kyle Russell, Jacque Zaremba, Larry Winderbaum, Paul Kelly, Roland Allen, Jon Reider, Team Evankovich, Julie Fenstermaker, Lauren Varacalli, Abu Noaman, Jason Putorti, Mark Exler, Daniel Steinmeyer, Jared Cohon, Gabriela Oates, Tri Ad Litho, David Koegler and Glen Meakem.

Bounce Back Team: Bryan Stokes II, John Lesjack, Emily Peters

College Prowler™
5001 Baum Blvd.
Suite 456
Pittsburgh, PA 15213

Phone: (412) 697-1390, 1(800) 290-2682
Fax: (412) 697-1396, 1(800) 772-4972
E-mail: info@collegeprowler.com
Website: www.collegeprowler.com

Welcome to College Prowler™

During the writing of College Prowler's guidebooks, we felt it was critical that our content was unbiased and unaffiliated with any college or university. We think it's important that our readers get honest information and a realistic impression of the student opinions on any campus — that's why if any aspect of a particular school is terrible, we (unlike a campus brochure) intend to publish it. While we do keep an eye out for the occasional extremist — the cheerleader or the cynic — we take pride in letting the students tell it like it is. We strive to create a book that's as representative as possible of each particular campus. Our books cover both the good and the bad, and whether the survey responses point to recurring trends or a variation in opinion, these sentiments are directly and proportionally expressed through our guides.

College Prowler guidebooks are in the hands of students throughout the entire process of their creation. Because you can't make student-written guides without the students, we have students at each campus who help write, randomly survey their peers, edit, layout, and perform accuracy checks on every book that we publish. From the very beginning, student writers gather the most up-to-date stats, facts, and inside information on their colleges. They fill each section with student quotes and summarize the findings in editorial reviews. In addition, each school receives a collection of letter grades (A through F) that reflect student opinion and help to represent contentment, prominence, or satisfaction for each of our 20 specific categories. Just as in grade school, the higher the mark the more content, more prominent, or more satisfied the students are with the particular category.

Once a book is written, additional students serve as editors and check for accuracy even more extensively. Our bounce-back team — a group of randomly selected students who have no involvement with the project — are asked to read over the material in order to help ensure that the book accurately expresses every aspect of the university and its students. This same process is applied to the 200-plus schools College Prowler currently covers. Each book is the result of endless student contributions, hundreds of pages of research and writing, and countless hours of hard work. All of this has led to the creation of a student information network that stretches across the nation to every school that we cover. It's no easy accomplishment, but it's the reason that our guides are such a great resource.

When reading our books and looking at our grades, keep in mind that every college is different and that the students who make up each school are not uniform — as a result, it is important to assess schools on a case-by-case basis. Because it's impossible to summarize an entire school with a single number or description, each book provides a dialogue, not a decision, that's made up of 20 different topics and hundreds of student quotes. In the end, we hope that this guide will serve as a valuable tool in your college selection process. Enjoy!

OMID GOHARI ○ CHRISTINA KOSHZOW ○ CHRIS MASON ○ JOEY RAHIMI ○ LUKE SKURMAN ○
The College Prowler™ Team

Table of Contents

Introduction from the Authors

When I go home to New York, people ask me where I go to college, and when I reply, "Kenyon," I inevitably get one of two responses. The first is a puzzled expression, to which I have to add "it's a small school in middle-of-nowhere Ohio." The latter group, which is the majority, know Kenyon for what it is: one of the premier small liberal arts schools in the country. If recent years are any indication, the group that hasn't heard of Kenyon is rapidly shrinking.

They know it for English and swimming, which is the school's traditional bread and butter, and while those areas remain strong, Kenyon is diversifying its strengths. Three years ago the school built a state-of-the-art $30 million science quad that has increased the proportion of science majors at Kenyon. Last Spring, the school broke ground on a $60 million athletic facility that will be among the best in Division III, and rival some Division I schools. The word is out. In just three years the admissions rate has gone from two-thirds to below 50 percent, and Kenyon is gaining the national recognition usually reserved for east coast schools with billion dollar endowments.

With all of these changes, one might think that Kenyon is a drastically different place then when Kenyon's founder and first president Bishop Philander Chase first climbed Gambier Hill in 1829. However, nothing could be further from the truth. When walking down Middle Path into "downtown" Gambier, one still feels as though it is a college nestled in nature fit for a Robert Frost poem. One hundred and seventy-five years later, the school has made some additions, namely women (including our first female president), telephones, and the Internet; however, the traditional feel remains the same. That's what Kenyon students love about their school. Other schools claim they are unique; Kenyon actually is.

I am here because my guidance counselor told me to go listen to a Kenyon recruiter. It was only when I made the trip to the place that maps forgot, and walked down Middle Path, that Kenyon's beauty had me hooked. I can't imagine life anywhere else. Kenyon is a school of learning and friendship. If this sounds like your cup of tea, hopefully this book can give you a few insights to life on the hill.

Jay Helmer and Zack Rosen
Authors
Kenyon College

By the Numbers

General Information
Kenyon College
Gambier, Ohio 43022

Control:
Private

Academic Calendar:
Semester

Religious Affiliation:
Episcopal

Founded:
1824

Website:
www.kenyon.edu

Main Phone:
(740) 427-5000

Admissions Phone:
(800) 848-2468

Student Body
**Full-Time
Undergraduates:**
1,592

**Part-Time
Undergraduates:**
20

**Total Male
Undergraduates:**
727

**Total Female
Undergraduates:**
885

Admissions

Overall Acceptance Rate:
46%

Early Decision Acceptance Rate:
84%

Regular Acceptance Rate:
44%

Total Applicants:
3,360

Total Acceptances:
1,534

Freshman Enrollment:
454

Yield (% of admitted students who actually enroll):
29.6%

Early Decision Available?
Yes

Early Action Available?
No

Regular Decision Deadline:
February 2

Regular Decision Notification:
April 1

Total Early Decision Applicants:
174

Total Early Decision Acceptances:
146

Early Decision One Deadline:
December 1

Early Decision One Notification:
December 17

Early Decision Two Deadline:
January 15

Early Decision Two Notification:
February 2

Must-Reply-By Date:
May 1

Common Application Accepted?
Yes

Supplemental Forms?
Yes

Admissions Phone:
(800) 848-2468

Admissions E-mail:
admissions@kenyon.edu

Admissions Website:
http://www.kenyon.edu/x602.xml

SAT I or ACT Required?
Yes

**SAT I Range
(25th – 75th Percentile):**
1220-1410

**SAT I Verbal Range
(25th – 75th Percentile):**
620 – 720

**SAT I Math Range
(25th – 75th Percentile):**
600-690

SAT II Requirements for Kenyon:
None required, although scores will be considered if submitted.

Retention Rate:
81%

**Top 10% of
High School Class:**
53%

Application Fee:
$45

Applicants Places on Waiting List:
580

Applicants Accepted From Waiting List:
212

Students Enrolled From Waiting List:
59

Trabsfer Applications Received:
116

Transfer Applications Accepted:
34

Transfer Students Enrolled:
17

Transfer Applicant Acceptance Rate:
29%

Financial Information

Full-Time Tuition:
$32,170

Room and Board:
$5,270

Books and Supplies for class:
$1,090

Average Need-Based Financial Aid Package:
$22,151

Students Who Applied For Financial Aid:
49%

Students Who Received Aid:
41%

Financial Aid Forms Deadline:
December 1

Financial Aid Phone:
(740) 427-5430

Financial Aid E-mail:
daugherty@kenyon.edu

Financial Aid Website:
http://www1.kenyon.edu/admissions/financial/

Academics

The Lowdown On...
Academics

Degrees Awarded:
Bachelor of Arts

Most Popular Areas of Study:
20% English language and literature/letters
20% social sciences
10% biological and biomedical sciences
10% visual and performing arts
9% multi/interdisciplinary studies

Full-Time Faculty:
168

Faculty with Terminal Degree:
99%

Student-to-Faculty Ratio:
9:1

Average Course Load:
Five classes

AP Test Score Requirements
Possible credit for scores of 3, 4 or 5

IB Test Score Requirements
Possible credit for scores of 6 or 7

Did You Know?

Sample Academic Clubs:
Math Club, Model UN, Debate Team

Best Places to Study
Gund Study Lounge, Library, Nu Phi Kappa in Ascension

Four-year graduation rate:
79%

Five-year graduation rate:
83%

Six-year graduation rate:
84%

Students Speak Out On...
Academics

"Kenyon has a lot to offer. Because it is a small school, and the student to faculty ratio is low, I think that in a lot of cases the faculty and administration are willing to bend over backwards for all of the students. It is a really hard school academically. Every syllabus of every class is jam-packed with all of the necessary reading and studying for that class. I've been pretty happy with every single class that I've taken."

Q "I cannot say enough good things about the faculty at Kenyon. They are among the brightest in their fields, and they are dedicated to teaching in a way that professors at research universities simply are not. **Academically, the faculty encourages students to be skeptical** and engaged learners, but their influence goes beyond the classroom. My faculty advisor took me out to lunch to convince me to study abroad; other faculty members have taken the time to help me find summer research positions and discuss the options I have after graduation. They are excellent scholars and totally dedicated to their students."

Q "I've enjoyed the majority of the classes I've taken here. The professors are knowledgeable and interested in the subject. They want you to succeed, and are generous with their time and energy in helping you reach academic goals. For the most part, I've gotten the classes I want. Registration is very easy and non-competitive. **Professors are often willing to sign for you to enter the class even if it's filled.**"

Q "It depends entirely on the student. **If you do all the homework and attempt to get something out of all the material, you will have an academic experience, and feel that you are working twice as hard as everyone else.** The academics are as difficult as you permit them to be, but as far as I understand, you actually have to work for an A, regardless of how intelligent you are. Not so for a B."

Q "Overall, the academics here are slightly below fantastic—slightly. The faculty rank as high as the academics. **The profs are great, but not the pre-eminent scholars in their field (for the most part).** The ability to get classes that you want is almost 100 percent, with the exception of English classes that fill up during major pre-enrollment."

Q "**The academics are wonderful!** No matter how difficult or easy your courses were in high school, Kenyon classes will challenge you to explore your horizons and think in new ways. The faculty is absolutely amazing here at Kenyon. They are outstanding scholars, and they also invest time and emotional commitment in their students. They really value you, the student, learning and understanding and enjoying, all at the same time. If you plan it right, you can get the classes you want. For really popular courses, there are usually several different sections and you should list alternate times, but I don't know anyone who didn't get a class. The teachers are also really nice about this. If you come to them and say I really want to take this course, they will usually let you add it."

Q "Overall, the academics are fantastic. Kenyon students often forget that, compared to ninety-five percent of colleges and universities, we have great teachers, challenging courses in a wide variety of subjects, and outstanding facilities. The faculty, though different from department to department, are dedicated, available, and engaging. **They are great people and a great resource.** Sometimes it can be difficult to get the classes you want, particularly in the larger departments or as a younger student, but it's not a serious problem."

Q "I don't think the academics at any institution could be that much better than what Kenyon has to offer. From the course selection, to the teachers, to the intimacy in the classroom, Kenyon's classes are extremely productive and very personal. The students and teachers are familiar with one another because there are at most fifteen students in most of my classes. I have incredible teachers in all of my classes, and **if I don't think that I understand a certain concept the teachers are always available for further discussion.** Fortunately I was able to get every class I wanted for my freshman year. Due to the size of the classes, certain classes are going to be more difficult to gain a spot, but I've been lucky to this point."

Q "It is fairly easy to get into introductory classes, but I wish that it was a little bit less selective and less hard to get into creative writing classes at Kenyon. **And the English department is really well-known.** I think that English majors really have to work hard to get into courses they are interested in because there is a lot of demand."

The College Prowler Take On...
Academics

It is easy to lose sight of the fact that Kenyon is a great academic school. The people are so nice and the campus is so scenic that people often forget just how hard everyone is working. A former president said that the Kenyon atmosphere is like "learning in the company of friends"; there seems to be little competition, even within majors and departments, but everyone spends a lot of time learning.

The traditional selling point of Kenyon College has been its English and Humanities program. Such esteemed writers as Robert Lowell and E.L. Doctorow were given their educations here, and Gambier is home to The Kenyon Review, one of the nations premier literary journals. English is by far the most populated major, and the scope of classes offered is far reaching. However, we are expanding from our English focus. The science quad and other changes have helped to rope in a wide range of majors. The humanities offer many classes. Kenyon's political science intro—The Quest for Justice—attracts many freshmen to the major, and the Integrated Program of Humane Studies (IPHS) gives first an overview of western literature and philosophy and then narrows down to more specific movements, such as post-modernism or romanticism. History and classics also attract many students, and the anthropology and sociology majors are also very popular. Kenyon prides itself on its small classes and close student/professor relationships. Faculty at Kenyon places their emphasis on teaching, as opposed to research. Every professor is required to hold at least five office hours a week. Kenyon does get many big name, high-profile professors on campus, but they are not treated any differently. They too have small classes and make themselves available, even if they did write "Eddie and the Cruisers."

A-

The College Prowler™ Grade on
Academics: A-

A high Academics grade generally indicates that professors are knowledgeable, accessible, and genuinely interested in their students' welfare. Other determining factors include class size, how well professors communicate, and whether or not classes are engaging.

Local Atmosphere

The Lowdown On...
Local Atmosphere

Region:
Midwest

City, State:
Gambier, Ohio

Setting:
Rural

Distance from Columbus:
1 Hour

Distance from Cleveland:
2 hours

→

Closest Shopping Malls or Plazas:

Easton Town Center

160 Easton Town Center

Columbus, OH 43219

(614) 416-7000

Closest Movie Theatres:

Premiere Theaters

Major Sports Teams:

Columbus Blue Jackets
(Hockey)
Columbus Crew
(Soccer)

City Websites

http://www.mountvernonohio.org

http://www.villageofgambier.org

Did You Know?

Four Fun Facts about Knox County:

- At nine stories, Kenyon's own Caples dormitory is the tallest building in the county.

- The New Testament Stone Garden in Mount Vernon illustrates fourteen bible passages through stones of various sizes, shapes, and weights.

- 1,110 privately owned, non-farm establishments employ 17,032 people in Knox County.

- The Village of Centerburg, Ohio, claims to be the exact geographical center of the state.

Local Slang

- **Sack**: a bag
- **Sketchy**: a person of ill repute
- **Copious**: a large amount of something (copious amounts of corn grow in Gambier)

Students Speak Out On...
Local Atmosphere

"Growing up in Long Island I was able to enjoy the mixture of both the city and country lifestyle. The village of Gambier is definitely not a metropolis, and that's what makes Kenyon so incredible. The students and faculty at Kenyon make up a large percentage of the residents in Gambier. Basically, Kenyon is the ideal college for anyone who enjoys the intimacy of a small town and isolation from the rest of the world. You can't always be isolated from the world though, and Mt. Vernon, only a five-minute drive from Gambier, allows Kenyon students to re-enter the lives they may have left. If you have the patience, you learn that Mt. Vernon has anything and everything you could want or need as a college student."

Q "Kenyon's location is definitely a plus because it is gorgeous. It's the perfect location for any student who wants to concentrate on their studies and have enough distractions to remain busy, but not too many to distort its students' priorities. The one thing all students must be aware of is that because of Kenyon's size, or lack there of, it's a very intense campus. **You will become familiar with almost everyone in your class, and you will be living with them for four years.** It helps a lot if you enjoy being around people!"

Q **"The village of Gambier is a charming addition to Kenyon's sense of community, as it reminds us that we are still members of society, despite the 'Kenyon Bubble.'** Everyday interactions with the post-office man, bookstore workers and bank members allow interactions that are not purely academic and force relationships that extend beyond college-age people. Mt. Vernon is adequate, although not terribly exciting, and I'd love to see more restaurants. At the same time, being so far from a major city allows us to participate in our own community in a bigger way. Location is positive, if you can handle the isolation. It gives a better focus to studies without distraction."

Q "Gambier is very cute and very pretty; **Mt. Vernon is very commercialized.** Kenyon's location is a positive and a negative, the quaint stuff is fun for a while, but in the end you do crave better food and more culture."

Q "Once you get beyond the initial 'middle of nowhere' factor, you really begin to love the village of Gambier. Cars stop for you, everything is really clean, and you are able to interact with other students, faculty, and residents every day just walking through. Mt. Vernon for what it is, a place to get all life's necessities, is fine. I actually like Gambier better, but Mt. Vernon is a fun random trip if you feel like it. Kenyon's location is definitely a positive. **Being surrounded by nature without a lot of distractions lets you get your work done and you're more likely to interact with other students more because you're not going into a city often.** Plus, Columbus isn't that far away at all, and there's a big shopping mecca only fifty-minutes away as well. Plus, it's just beautiful here."

Q "I came out to Kenyon to visit and I pretty much knew what Kenyon was going to be like, and I think that you don't come to Kenyon looking for a city. You don't come to Kenyon looking for a Gap or J. Crew on the corner. That is what part of the beauty of Kenyon is. **The fact that it is in around a beautiful rural landscape, and it has a lot to offer with its small community as far as community service and reporting for the newspaper.** There are a lot of ways students can really work with their surroundings, whereas in the big city they might feel that they are unable to make a difference."

Q "The village of Gambier is incredibly small and quaint. There really isn't too much to it. Mt. Vernon is kind of hickish with a lot of Mennonites and 'middle-America' restaurants and stores. Kenyon's location is very isolated but that's what I like about it. **It's a break from reality. Plus, Columbus is only fifty-minutes away.**"

Q "Gambier is very picturesque and quiet. Mt. Vernon is a good place to get away. Mt. Vernon has all the staples like McDonald's and Wal-Marts, movie theatres, and bowling alleys, and also a pretty, historical section of town. I think Kenyon's location is a positive. If you're from a big city, it takes a little adjusting (my best friend said that there are more people in two blocks in Chicago than in the entire town of Gambier including students), but there's always Columbus if you love crowds and traffic. **The quietness of Gambier is conducive to studying**—there aren't a whole lot of procrastinating excuses in the town itself."

Q "**The village of Gambier is perhaps the world's greatest college town**—it's only a touch too small. As far as Mt. Vernon—if it weren't for Wal-Mart and Kroger, our hickish sense of civilization would be totally useless. Kenyon's location is an extreme positive. Simply put: Kenyon would not function at all outside of Gambier."

Q "Gambier and Knox County are what make Kenyon what it is, plain and simple, and for better and for worse. Don't come here if you're looking for great nightlife opportunities, world-class theatres or art, or hustle and bustle. That said, **there are incredible opportunities here that you won't get in a larger campus setting**: the chance to spend a lot of time with a small group of people in a beautiful rural environment."

The College Prowler Take On...
Local Atmosphere

When other people complain about how small their college town is, Kenyon students just roll their eyes. While Kenyon students are very modern, everything around them looks like a time warp. Bustling downtown Gambier is a single block long, and features a market, deli, bookstore, coffee shop, post office, bar, and barber. The Amish sell crafts and produce in the fall, and sometimes a guy sells jewelry and sweaters outside of Farr hall. Before you judge this scene, I should say that Kenyon students love it. Gambier functions as a blank canvas for Kenyon students. It is simple, slow and quiet, and any student activity stands out all the more against this backdrop. You get so used to this so quickly that even a visit to Mount Vernon can seem jarring. If all this becomes too much to bare, there is a fair amount to do in the surrounding towns and counties. If you like things that are quaint and pretty, then you will be set. Apple picking, haunted houses, blue grass festivals, and homemade pie can all be found within a thirty minute drive of Kenyon. If you want to drive a little further than that (say, an hour), Columbus offers culture, restaurants, and a variety of other non-collegiate diversions. Ten minutes outside the city is the Easton shopping center, which is about as big as Kenyon and has a Cheesecake Factory, a Gap, and its own street signs. Any feelings of missing modern culture and convenience will be quickly wiped away by the shiny suburban monstrosity.

All in all, the thing to stress most about Kenyon's local atmosphere is to know what you are getting in to. Students who transfer after their freshman year are the ones who thought they could force themselves to like what Kenyon is. The happiest students are the ones that knew they were going to a small school in the cornfields and looked forward to it anyway.

The College Prowler™ Grade on

Local Atmosphere: C+

A high Local Atmosphere grade indicates that the area surrounding campus is safe and scenic. Other factors include nearby attractions, proximity to other schools, and the town's attitude toward students

Safety & Security

The Lowdown On...
Safety & Security

Number of Kenyon Police:

16

Kenyon Security Phone:

(740) 427-5109

Safety Services:

Transportation, escort service, engraving, campus watch, safety whistles

Health Services:

Basic medical services, counseling services

Health Center Office Hours

Monday-Friday 9 a.m. - 4:30 a.m.

Students Speak Out On...
Safety & Security

"I started out as a freshman feeling as if security was always out to get me. Whether or not I was throwing a party in my room or going to a party, I always felt as if they were the enemy. As I have gone on and now am a senior, I appreciate their role; I realize they are not out to get us. They have done a lot for the school, and at least 90 percent of the time they care about the good of the students."

Q "**Safety and Security seem to be sort of malicious.** They don't act like they're here for our safety. They act like they're bitter and want to get people in trouble because they can."

Q "Safety and Security's role is to **hassle students**, and to occasionally provide a **helpful service.** They are a presence."

Q "Safety and Security crack down a lot on parties, but I don't think they're too strict. **You can always call them for a ride home**, and people take advantage of that, which is good. (They don't always do that at other schools.)"

Q "I'm not too familiar with the Safety and Security department, but I do know **they've always been there whenever our fire alarm has gone off** (around fifteen times in two months), and they are always efficient with towing cars when you leave your car alone for too long. Fortunately, I'm not too familiar with the Safety and Security personnel, but I did go on the campus lighting walk, which I think is an incredible idea, as an electrician a couple security officers and students walk around the campus finding areas that are too dark. So far I'm satisfied, and from what I've heard from the lighting walk, there are plenty of safety projects that will make the students feel even more comfortable, which is never a concern anyway."

Q "**The campus at large is very safe,** and although lighting is a concern, most girls, I believe, feel comfortable walking alone at night."

Q "In practice, it is a truly nice convenience to be able to visit any dorm, especially at odd hours, without having to be buzzed in. **Being such a small community the unlocked doors rarely elicits unwelcome visitors aside from the occasional wandering drunk.** The doors to individual rooms can obviously be locked for privacy and safety."

The College Prowler Take On...
Safety & Security

My freshman year, my resident advisor scheduled a hall meeting and wouldn't tell us what it was for. She would only say it was a surprise and it would be worth it for us to come. This meeting ended up being a presentation by one of the security guards, a very nice woman named Melanie. She passed out cookies and cool whip and went over some basic policies of the school. She just wanted us to be safe and not get in trouble. Kenyon is about as non-threatening as a school can get. Dorms and academic buildings stay unlocked and people leave their backpacks unattended for hours at the library. Kenyon is an incredibly safe and trusting environment. The thefts that do happen are almost impossible to trace because they are a product of trust. People steal unlocked bikes, food in community refrigerators, and shoes from unlocked lockers.

Security is there mostly as party monitors. They check to make sure underage students aren't drinking and that everything is up to fire code. During the day they can be seen riding around campus in their SUVs, but there is not much for them to do. Party nights they go through dorms and check on loud rooms, but a little common sense (no blasting music and no one screaming "I'm so drunk!") will ensure that you stay out of trouble in this respect. Security truly does care about the students. Being a 2,000-person village, Gambier doesn't really have any dark alleys or bad neighborhoods. A lot of campus is poorly lit, but there are committees debating that fact all the time, and blue security phones are visible in all the less populated areas. Most of the people that hang out around Kenyon are Kenyon students.

A

The College Prowler™ Grade on

Safety & Security: A

A high grade in Safety & Security means that students generally feel safe, campus police are visible, blue-light phones and escort services are readily available, and safety precautions are not overly necessary.

Computers

The Lowdown On...
Computers

High-Speed Network?
Yes.

Wireless Network?
Yes, in dorms

Number of Labs:
10

Number of Computers:
173

Operating Systems:
Windows 2000, NT

Discounted Software

None

Free Software

None

24-Hour Labs

Gund Study Lounge, Roth Lab in the basement of Pierce, Labs in the basement of Ascension.

Charge to Print?

No

Students Speak Out On...
Computers

"There are a ton of computers. I think it is nice to have a computer. I don't think it is absolutely necessary. If you are going to bring a computer, it is nice to have a laptop because it gives you the flexibility of going to the library with it—it also gives you the flexibility of finding an empty classroom or study room where you can use it. But I don't think it is absolutely necessary, but I think that it may be in the future. I think that Kenyon has done a pretty good job of trying to supply 24-hour computer access to students, and I have had very little trouble finding a free computer at pretty much every hour during the day."

"The computers are pretty good. Freshmen all live in roughly the same area and Gund Commons has enough for everybody. It's definitely nice to have one in your room, if you can control yourself. **Meaning, if you have work to do, will having a computer in your room make you gravitate to the sports news or solitaire?** Doing work in the library or a computer lab limits your procrastinating excuses."

"The college is gradually moving towards replacing the poor computers that still exist in the basement of Ascension and other random areas around campus. **The sciences are mostly covered, while the humanities are somewhat lacking.** Throughout campus there are almost enough computers, although the library should definitely have more. I would advise bringing a personal computer, if only for personal convenience."

Q "The campus' computers are top-of-the-line. There are more than enough computers on campus to satisfy the student body because enough students bring their own computers. I brought my computer and it's really been helpful, but in case my laptop crashed I would never have a problem finding another computer to use, even if it's a fellow dorm mates. **I think it would be beneficial for any student to have a computer because** it would make your life a lot easier since it's so convenient to setup a computer in your dorm, and just work from home instead of walking a couple minutes away. I don't know, you can definitely survive without a computer, but if you're attached to the Internet, go ahead and bring one."

Q "While there are computers available all over campus, it's best to bring one for personal use as things can get crowded especially around finals. **The connections are fast, wireless is coming into certain campus buildings, and the support is available and thorough.**"

Q "The campus computers are fine, although I barely ever use them. **One should definitely bring his or her own computer.** If everybody relied on the campus labs, all hell would break loose."

Q "I use my own computer. There seem to be enough in the library and other facilities, but **it gets pretty crowded around midterms, finals, and Sunday nights.** Your own laptop is necessary at that point."

Q "The computing system at Kenyon has strengths and pitfalls. On the plus side, **there is Internet access for every student in his/her room, and 100-MB on the school server for each student to store files.** There is also a student run Napster server that makes it possible to download virtually any song in a matter of seconds. The downside is reliability. The student drives on the server are often difficult to access from computer labs, and the email server is faulty a couple of times a week."

Q "With the exception of exam time, **Kenyon has ample computer lab space.** While the computers on the main floor of the library may be difficult to snag in evening hours, the computer labs in the basement of buildings are generally available. Exam time, however, is a different animal."

Q "For the majority of the year **it is possible to survive without one**; however, most students prefer to have the regular access to e-mail and IM that a PC allows."

The College Prowler Take On...
Computers

Like most colleges, the majority of Kenyon students own their own computers. The school provides Ethernet hookup in every room, and a blue cord that connects you both to the net and to the Kenyon network. E-mail is used often here, both for personal correspondence and college business, so being able to check your mail at your leisure is very nice. A student's room may prove to be the last place they would be able to work in peace. That is why a lot of students, even the aforementioned computer owners, do their work at many of the computer labs scattered around campus. In general there are enough computers, and students stagger their study hours, that you will be able to find one if you need one. The more popular locations, like the library and Gund Commons, fill up quickly, but there are many "secret" computer labs scattered around campus. The basement of Ascension hall has two such labs, as does Pierce hall.

The only time the computer situation gets a little hairy is during finals. At this time, students come out of the woodworks to write their papers, and the competition for computers gets fierce. It is during these times that you will either stick to your own computer or be very crafty about getting an open one in the lab. Gund Commons will be a lost cause—it is not uncommon to see someone camped out there for days at a time, sometime with a pillow and blanket for naps. The library is also very difficult. Your best bet at these times is Pierce or Sam Mather.

B-

The College Prowler™ Grade on

Computers: B-

A high grade in Computers designates that computer labs are available, the computer network is easily accessible, and the campus' computing technology is up-to-date.

Facilities

The Lowdown On...
Facilities

Student Center:
The middle of town is Kenyon's student center, but the closest thing we have is Gund Commons

Athletic Center:
Ernst Center

Libraries:
1

Popular Places to Chill:
The patio in front of Farr hall, the bookstore

Campus size:
1,200 acres

What Is There to Do On Campus?

During the week, you can work in the library, go jogging down the Kokosing Gap Trail, or swim laps at Ernst athletic center. At night there is a plethora of Kenyon-sponsored "dry events" to compliment the drinking and Greek scene.

Movie Theatre on Campus?

No

Bowling on Campus?

No

Bar on Campus?

Gambier Grille (behind the bookstore)

Coffeehouse on Campus?

Middle Ground

Favorite Things to Do:

A lot of Kenyon's favorite activities involve simply hanging out with friends. Whether you park your scooters in the Gund patio or sit in the benches outside Farr, the school very often resembles an admissions booklet. Students sit and read magazines in the bookstore, study as groups in the library atrium, and hold hands on the bench at Sunset Point. When it snows, people sled down hills on lunch trays. There is always some event to go see, whether it is a student-produced, senior-thesis play, improv and sketch comedy, or a speaker. The campuses three a cappella groups are immensely popular: the concerts are always packed, and students will go out of the way to see them do teaser sets at various coffee houses and fundraisers. The Kenyon Film Society (KFS) designates a theme every week (musicals, black and white, Sean Penn) and shows three movies a week on Wednesday, Friday, and Saturday. Sporting events can usually reel in some spectators, depending on the sport and the weather, and any event offering free food pretty much guarantees attendance.

Students Speak Out On...
Facilities

"Is Kenyon's lack of a student union a good thing?—No. Gund Commons is close, although nowhere near adequate. It's fantastic, although I have a hard time believing the average student goes there seven times a day. With the exception of the science quad, the school buildings are for the most part beautiful from the outside, and in need of a major overhaul on the inside, especially the historic South dorms, and especially Leonard of those three."

Q "The architecture is amazing, but the insides of the buildings aren't all that great. I am a little bit afraid of the student union that is being built right now at the bottom of our hill. I am afraid that it might take away from the role that the town now plays as a sort of a student union, as a meeting place for the student and move it down to the bottom of the hill. I think that is a real problem, but at the same time Kenyon is in need of good athletic facilities. I think that one of the biggest problems Kenyon has is that there is a very cold winter, and people still need to exercise. **Not having enough indoor exercise facilities for the student body is not good for average student health.** I think that exercise is good for mental and physical health. Really we do need more exercise facilities down at the bottom of the hill or some place, but we don't necessarily need a student union because I think that the library, Pierce, Town, Gund Commons in any season is a fine and a good meeting point. It also adds to the uniqueness of the campus."

Q "The village is a part of the college, and only time will tell how much the village will play a part in my Kenyon experience. **Basically you will become familiar with all the**

faces in town and there will be an understood unity that is found in any small town."

Q "The bookstore is one of the best you will find in the nation. It's a place to study, hang out, and it has anything and everything you would ever want or need. **I'd still buy my books off of Amazon.com,** but the bookstore has everything and a wonderful staff. Some of the school buildings may have been built close to two centuries ago, but you wouldn't notice it. Every building is comfortable and well furnished. I lived in a dorm with carpeting and air conditioning as a freshman! What more can I ask for. The classrooms are wonderful and the buildings some of your lectures are in were once homes, and it's just awesome at times when you realize how special of a place Kenyon is. Round-table discussions in almost every class and plenty of opinions to share make up good times!"

Q "**The bookstore is amazing.** The buildings are beautiful. I love Ascension."

Q "**The academic facilities, particularly in the sciences, are excellent.** We have some beautiful classrooms, more historic buildings than you can shake a stick at, and several good performance spaces. The art facilities could use some work, and while there are a few exceptional residences, student housing is fairly primitive. The lack of a student union is not a problem. Gambier's various gathering spaces serve the purpose more than adequately."

Q "The back of the bookstore is an excellent study area. It's also **one of the few places you'll find cute guys** on this campus—I'm serious."

Q "At first I thought it was kind of weird that we didn't have a student union, but now I can't picture Kenyon with one. We interact so much in our dorms and classes that you don't really need a student union. **The buildings are beautiful, clean, and pretty modern.**"

Q "The village is pretty much the equivalent of a student union. **Also, the new gym facility will help in that area.** The bookstore is a great place to hang out and study. The dorms are very seventies-ish, which I don't like so much. The academic buildings are nice, and Ascension is very classic."

The College Prowler Take On...
Facilities

Kenyon is very proud of the fact that we have no student union. The truth is, we don't need one. The entire village is built around students, and the campus is not big enough for us to lose track of each other without a central meeting place. Downtown Gambier serves as the center of student life, and the bookstore is the campuses heartbeat. Everything from shampoo to staple guns to gummy bears is sold there (books of course are too), and there are comfy chairs in every corner. It is very easy to kill two hours in the bookstore without realizing it. You get a bagel, a cup of tea, and a stack of new magazines and time just flies. Most building on campus are never locked, so there are a plethora of available meeting spaces. The library atrium is one of the most popular, as is the Gund Commons ballroom. Every building on campus is extremely inviting. The majority of the ones on south campus look like castles, and the ones that don't (the library, Ernst) are at least cozy enough to be inviting.

A huge complaint on campus is the lackluster athletic facilities, but this will be remedied with the construction of the new fitness and recreation center. This $60 million building is to feature a pool, tennis court, indoor track, and pro shop. Rosse hall is the main venue for speakers and large scale musical performances. Behind it is the smaller Storer hall, which functions as a rehearsal space for the campus orchestra and a venue for smaller performances. On North Campus, Bexley Hall is where the majority of art classes are taught, and the nearby "art barn," containing all sculpture and painting facilities, is where the art majors live during finals time. The Bolton dance studio accommodates the small number of dance majors, and our two theaters are reserved for all plays and drama classes.

The College Prowler™ Grade on

Facilities: C

A high Facilities grade indicates that the campus is aesthetically pleasing and well-maintained; facilities are state-of-the-art, and libraries are exceptional. Other determining factors include the quality of both athletic and student centers and an abundance of things to do on campus.

Campus Dining

The Lowdown On...
Campus Dining

Freshman Meal Plan Requirement?
Yes

Off-Campus Places to Use Your Meal Plan
None

Meal Plan Average Cost:
$3,040

24-Hour On-Campus Eating?
None

→

→

Places to Grab a Bite with Your Meal Plan

Gund Servery
Location: Gund Commons
Food: all types
Favorite Dish: Chicken Parmesan

Pierce Hall
Location: Gund Commons
Food: all types
Favorite Dish: Thanksgiving

Philander's Pub
Location: Gund Commons
Food: all types
Favorite Dish: Pizza

Students Speak Out On...
Campus Dining

"Campus dining could be worse and seems to be improving. The dining service managers are extremely receptive to student input, and try very hard to provide for everyone and supply us with a great deal of daily options. With a little creativity one can put together decent, healthy meals in the dining halls."

Q "The food is good enough for me. I guess it's good that the food isn't incredible, so I don't put on any extra weight, but it's never awful. Sometimes it's a little repetitive, but there's always a variety of foods to choose from in both Gund and Pierce. **RFOC was cool at first, but it's not always great,** but there are always a few pearls offered."

Q "Quality of campus dining? Ha—right! Good joke. It could be worse, I suppose, but for 37,000 a year it could be a hell of a lot better. **There is a consistent lack of options.** I don't think too many students will fight over that one. As far as RFOC, more like Real bad Food On Campus. With the exception of the meat carving station, it's ARAMark with a daily helping of hamburgers."

Q "It's a typical college dining service. **Not great, but not disgusting.** As far as RFOC, it was good for the first few weeks, but then it got old."

Q "Surprisingly I really do love the food here. **I think most college students expect to go out to eat when they go to the dining hall or something.** Kenyon doesn't have tons of options sometimes, but for the most part, it's all really good."

Q "**Dining has really improved.** The 'scramble system' is great if you're not scared of 'cutting' people in line. The pub downstairs offers subs, pizza, and pasta. The all you can eat and extend-o hours are very convenient."

Q "The twenty-one meal plan courtesy of Aramark food service is automatically a part of the Kenyon education. The general consensus of the student body is that the quality of the food leaves much to be desired. **It is possible to sustain oneself on the food, but gaining the 'freshman fifteen' from the dining hall food is not a concern**."

Q "Occasionally a meal such as chicken patties will entice the general populations' appetites, but those are rare. **Attempts to add flavor to a generally plain menu are often overdone**, and leave it nearing the inedible threshold."

Q "Gambier itself offers a precious few alternatives to the blandness of Aramark. The Gambier Deli makes a pretty good sandwich but its prices, ($7-$10) make it impossible for them to be a regular part of a student's diet. The Gambier Grill, whose primary function is the campuses only real bar, makes decent grill type food at an affordable price. **There is also the Kenyon Inn, which serves legitimate three-star gourmet food**, but prices ($40-$50 a head) generally make it an option only when one's parents are in town."

Q "I think that students are always going to complain about food. I think that they are doing a lot to change the food at Kenyon. **They are doing a good job, it is improving.** It is tough because it is such a social point of the day where everyone wants to go to Pierce, and not as many people want to go to Gund anymore, so I think that's a downer, but I think that at the same time, for Kenyon, dinner has always been really important. As long as students feel comfortable going into Pierce or Gund and finding food that they like and that they can eat, the better. I see it as a great time during the day where I can catch up with my friends that I wouldn't necessarily see elsewhere. You really realize how small and comfortable the size of the student body is when you walk into Pierce, and you can pretty much know you are going to bump into one of your friends."

The College Prowler Take On...
Campus Dining

Kenyon is one of the last schools in the country where anyone can simply walk in and eat a meal. This is because we have no meal plan. You go to Kenyon, you eat as much as you want for as long as you want. Before you get excited, just remember this plan is born out of desperation, not convenience. If a Kenyon student stops eating in the cafeteria, they are either going to starve or go broke within days. It is not that our food is bad. As college food goes, it is actually pretty decent. The problem at Kenyon lies in familiarity. You will get to know all the campus food options very well, very soon. That is why the school, in conjunction with ARAMARK, the campus food server, recently kicked off the Real Food On Campus initiative. RFOC, as it is commonly known, attempts to add flavor and diversity to the dining experience, all in hopes of making it resemble "real food."

In some ways, it has been successful. Every day they offer burgers (both beef and veggie), hot dogs, fries and grilled cheese or chicken patties as an alternative. There is always an entrée' du jour, usually a meat dish, a pasta dish, and a complimentary vegetable. There is also a salad bar, soup, and cereal at all meals. Pierce Hall has the added bonus of PanGeos, which is various regional dishes (Oriental noodles, Mediterranean wraps) cooked up fresh in front of you. The lines for these are usually very long, but it can be well worth your wait. Pierce is where the majority of the upperclassmen eat, and in general the more popular servery for its options and atmosphere. Gund offers everything above (except pangeos), but is on North Campus, and is frequented almost exclusively by non-athletes, freshmen and north dwelling upperclassmen. It is more of a "homey" servery, where as Pierce is a little more of a social scene.

B-

The College Prowler™ Grade on
Campus Dining: B-

Our grade on Campus Dining addresses the quality of both school-owned dining halls and independent on-campus restaurants as well as the price, availability, and variety of food.

Off-Campus Dining

The Lowdown On...
Off-Campus Dining

Restaurant Prowler: Popular Places to Eat!

- Alcove, 116 South Main Street, steaks, chops, sandwiches, salads, bar service, (740) 392-3076.
- Bob Evans, 857 Coshocton Avenue, American, breakfast all day, sausage from Bob Evans Farms, 740-393-1700.
- Curtis Inn on the Square, 12 Public Square, American, hamburgers, sandwiches, bar service, 740-397-4334.
- Fiesta Mexicana, 308 West High Street, Mexican, bar service, 740-397-6325.
- Flappers Bar and Grill, 15 West High Street, steaks, chicken, pasta, sandwiches, bar service, 740-392-1061.
- Friendly's Ice Cream Shop, 803 Coshocton Avenue, hamburgers, sandwiches, ice cream specialties, breakfasts, 740-397-6589.
- Golden City, 216 South Main Street, oriental and American, bar service, 740-397-1282.
- Henry's, 12 Public Square, American, hamburgers, sandwiches, bar service, 740-397-4334.

→

- Hunan Garden, 1516 Coshocton Avenue, authentic Hunan and Szechuan food, 740-393-1313.
- Jake's, 996 Coshocton Ave, American, salads, steaks, sandwiches, 740-397-1418.
- Jody's, 109 South Main Street, American, sandwiches, breakfast anytime, 740-397-9573.
- La Paloma, 856 Coshocton Avenue, Mexican, 740-393-4101.
- Mazza's Ristorante, 214 West High Street, Italian, bar service, 740-393-2076.
- The Parkside, 108 Mt. Vernon Avenue, 740-427-4131.
- Pizza Hut, pizza, sandwiches, beer, 1061 Coshocton Avenue, 740-397-2275, and South Main Street (corner of Kirk Street), 740-392-6110.
- R&M's Southside Diner, 620 South Main Street, fifties-style diner with American food and some Greek specialties, 740-392-1282.
- Ruby Tuesday, 1055 Coshocton Avenue, chicken, hamburgers, pasta, steaks, salad bar, 740-397-5410.
- Ryan's, 1485 Coshocton Avenue, steaks, salad bar, 740-397-5410.
- Sip's Cafe, 124 S. Main Street, coffee, baked goods, soups and sandwiches, 740-392-2233.

Fast food (all Mount Vernon)
- Arby's, 1057 Coshocton Avenue, 740-392-5010.
- Burger King, 9 Martinsburg Road, 740-397-8644.
- Donato's Pizza, 221 West High Street, 740-397-3336.
- Hardee's, 856 Coshocton Avenue, 740-397-8931.
- Kentucky Fried Chicken, 301 West High Street, 740-392-4900.
- Little Caesar's Pizza, 9 North Sandusky Street, 740-393-1865.
- Long John Silver's, 935 Coshocton Avenue, 740-397-6787.
- McDonald's, 111 Newark Road, 740-397-5501, and 1059 Coshocton Avenue, 397-5503.
- Papa John's Pizza, 855 Coshocton Avenue, 740-397-6644.
- Subway, 1558 Coshocton Avenue, 740-392-8338.
- Taco Bell, 1015 Coshocton Avenue, 740-393-3133.
- Wendy's, 522 South Main Street, 740-397-3440, and 944 Coshocton Avenue, 740-397-3407.

Best Pizza:
Gambier Grille

Best Chinese:
Hunan

Best Breakfast:
Jody's

Best Wings:
Jake's

Best Place to Take Your Parents
Kenyon Inn

Closest Grocery Store
Kroger

Students Speak Out On...
Off-Campus Dining

"There aren't an awful lot of off-campus dining options after 10 or 11 at night. However, there are a few options in Mt. Vernon and in those cases you really do need a car. There's one spot on campus right now, there is another one being built, there's the bookstore for snacks, but really for dinner you might be able to pick up a sandwich at the deli, but other than that it is a little bit harder to find food after 11 o'clock."

Q "Off-campus options, with a few notable exceptions (the Kenyon Inn, Middle Ground, Deli), are slim: mediocre Mexican, soupy Chinese, fast food, and enough diners to harden the arteries of a 1,500-strong student body with grease left over for the faculty and administration. Fortunately, **Jody's Restaurant has unbelievable breakfast specials, and Kroger is open all night.**"

Q "**Off-campus dining is pretty limited to crappy food** like Friendly's, McDonald's, etc. The deli on campus is good."

Q "There are not so many off-campus dining options close to campus. You either need to **have a car, or have a friend who has a car**, to get to any good restaurants. Anything at Easton is good."

Q "If you go into town, there are enough off-campus dining opportunities, especially if you are married to your favorite fast food chain. If not, it's basically Ruby Tuesday, Jakes, the Alcove and Fiesta. **Jakes and The Alcove are the best.** Jakes is like Applebee's (or a similar chain) whereas the Alcove probably touches $20/meal including drinks, excluding dessert."

Q "Mt. Vernon has several options for food, and there are some relative roses, among the thorns of fast food. The most popular is a restaurant called Jakes, which serves quality **American-style food, with a pleasant atmosphere and for a very reasonable price.**"

Q "About twenty minutes drive from Gambier, is Peggy Sue's, which is a little known, but **very good home style restaurant** where one can get a big meal for $10."

The College Prowler Take On...
Off-Campus Dining

Because your meal plan only covers the three places listed above, everything else, regardless of location, will be considered off-campus. The best option for local dining is the Gambier Deli. It offers very good sandwiches and other deli options, and is open until 8 p.m., Monday through Saturday. The typical meal there will cost somewhere around $8, though, which can be a little pricey for a student's budget. The Gambier Grill offers burgers, chicken wings and the like, but the food is eaten mostly as late-night delivery. The Grill's main function is as the campus bar. The newly-opened Middle Ground will serve as a coffee and lunch spot, and may become a pleasant alternative to what ARAMARK has to offer. The best local dining is at the Kenyon Inn, but at $50 a head, it is usually seen only during parental visits and very special occasions. The Kenyon Inn is the only place in Gambier that you will ever see a table-cloth.

For those with a car, the real dining options are in Mount Vernon—if it's cheap, or a chain, it's in Vernon. There is fast food, such as McDonalds, Wendy's, Taco Bell, and KFC, and then there are the chains, such as Friendly's, Bob Evans, Ruby Tuesday, and Arby's. There are several restaurants in Mount Vernon that fall into neither of these categories, and they are actually quite good. Jake's is a place for steak, and can be a little expensive when ordering its feature item, but also has great burgers at a much lower price. Jodie's serves gigantic pancakes all day and is my only viable breakfast option. The Southside diner has 24-hour breakfast, as does the High Street Diner. Hunan Garden, probably the most frequented of the non-chain restaurants, is also the best. It serves Chinese food and should not be missed.

The College Prowler™ Grade on

Off-Campus Dining: C

A high off-campus dining grade implies that off-campus restaurants are affordable, accessible, and worth visiting. Other factors include the variety of cuisine and the availability of alternative options (vegetarian, vegan, Kosher, etc.).

Campus Housing

The Lowdown On...
Campus Housing

Room Types:
Standard, share bathrooms on floor or wing

Suite style: a set of rooms adjoined by a common room

Private: private bathrooms or share with one other person

Apartment: suite style rooms with a shared bathroom per apartment

Best Dorms:
Tafts, Manning,

Worst Dorms:
Caples, Leonard

→

Dormitories

Bushnell Residence Hall

Floors: 2+ basement

Total Occupancy: 51

Bathrooms: two per wing

Co-Ed: No

Percentage of Men/Women: 0%/100%

Percentage of First-Year Students: 1%

Room Types: Standard

Special Features: Large main lounge with TV and cable, Kitchen in basement, Carpeted hallway, Window blinds, Moveable furniture, Large student storage room

Caples Residence Hall

Floors: 9+ basement

Total Occupancy: 146

Bathrooms: two per floor

Co-Ed: Yes

Percentage of Men/Women: 42%/58%

Percentage of First-Year Students: 2%

Room Types: Standard, Suite

Special Features: Kitchen on first-floor, TV lounge with Cable, Laundry Facility in basement, fully carpeted rooms and hallways, limited furniture provided in suite lounges, adjustable heating and air conditioning, movable furniture, Venetian blinds.

Farr Residence Hall

Floors: 1

Total Occupancy: 34

Bathrooms: Singles share adjoining bathroom, doubles have private bathroom

Co-Ed: Yes

Percentage of Men/Women: 47%/53%

Percentage of First-Year Students: 0%

Room Types: premium, Suite

Special Features: New Furniture, Cable Availability, full carpeted, two-person apartments have bathroom and kitchenette: includes 2 burner stove, sink refrigerator

Gund Residence Hall

Floors: 2+ basement

Total Occupancy: 81

Bathrooms: one per wing

Co-Ed: Yes

Percentage of Men/Women: 55%/45%

Room Types: standard

Special Features: Venetian blinds, large lounge with television, laundry facility in basement, study lounges on each floor, exercise facility, built in room dividers featuring a bookshelf and bulletin board, built in furniture and storage compartments.

Hanna Residence Hall

Floors: 3+ basement

Total Occupancy: 78

Bathrooms: four per floor

Co-Ed: Yes

Percentage of Men/Women: 53%/47%

Percentage of First-Year Students: 95%

Room Types: Standard

Special Features: Large Rooms, large windows with Venetian blinds, fully carpeted rooms and hallways, lounges include TV with cable

Leonard Residence Hall

Floors: 4+ basement

Total Occupancy: 93

Bathrooms: two per floor

Co-Ed: Yes

Percentage of Men/Women: 65%/35%

Percentage of First-Year Students: 0%

Room Types: Standard

Special Features: Bay Window, Several windows in doubles, rooms and hallway carpeted, large doubles, lounges with Cable TV

Lewis Residence Hall

Floors: 2

Total Occupancy: 83

Bathrooms: one per wing

Co-Ed: Yes

Percentage of Men/Women: 53%/47%

Percentage of First-Year Students: 91%

Room Types: Standard

Special Features: Venetian blinds with recessed curtain rods, movable furniture, built in wardrobes, lounge with cable TV, microwave oven, vending machine

Manning Residence Hall

Floors: 2+ basement

Total Occupancy: 51

Bathrooms: two per wing

Co-Ed: Yes

Percentage of Men/Women: 48%/52%

Percentage of First-Year Students: 0%

Room Types: Standard,

Special Features: movable furniture, Venetian blinds, laundry facility in basement, kitchen area on first floor, large TV lounge with Cable, ping pong table, study lounge with internet ports in basement, study lounge with internet ports in basement carpeted hallways.

Mather Residence Hall

Floors: 4+ basement

Total Occupancy: 177

Bathrooms: two per floor

Co-Ed: Yes

Percentage of Men/Women: 56%/44%

Percentage of First-Year Students: 31%

Room Types: Standard

Special Features: movable furniture, Venetian blinds, laundry facility in basement, kitchen area, fully carpeted, large TV lounge with Cable, adjustable heating and air conditioning,

vending machines

McBride Residence Hall

Floors: 3+basement

Total Occupancy: 184

Bathrooms: Two per floor

Co-Ed: Yes

Percentage of Men/Women: 42%/58%

Percentage of First-Year Students: 95%

Room Types: standard

Special Features: movable furniture, Venetian blinds, laundry facility in basement, kitchen area, fully carpeted, large TV lounge with Cable, adjustable heating and air conditioning, vending machines

Norton Residence Hall

Floors: 2

Total Occupancy: 78

Bathrooms: One per wing

Co-Ed: Yes

Percentage of Men/Women: 44%/56%

Percentage of First-Year Students: 94%

Room Types: Standard

Special Features: Venetian blinds with recessed curtain rods, movable furniture, built in wardrobes, lounge with cable TV, microwave oven, vending machine

Old Kenyon Residence Hall

Floors: 4+ basement

Total Occupancy: 144

Bathrooms: two per floor

Co-Ed: Yes

Percentage of Men/Women: 56%/44%

Percentage of First-Year Students: 0%

Room Types: Standard

Special Features: movable furniture, Venetian blinds, laundry facility in basement, microwave in basement, 4 large TV lounges in basement, patios, study lounge with table in basement, fully carpeted rooms and hallways, student storage on forth floor.

Watson Residence Hall

Floors: 2+ basement

Total Occupancy: 43

Bathrooms: one per floor

Co-Ed: Yes

Percentage of Men/Women: 58%/42%

Percentage of First-Year Students: 0%

Room Types: Standard

Special Features: movable furniture, Venetian blinds, laundry facility in basement, kitchen on first floor, carpeted hallways, large TV lounge with Cable, built in wardrobes

Acland Apartments

Total Occupancy: 48

Bathrooms: One bathroom in each six- person apartment

Co-Ed: Yes

Percentage of Men/Women:

37%/63%

Percentage of First-Year Students: 0%

Room Types: Standard but with a very large common room

Special Features: Stove, Oven small refrigerator

Bexley Apartments

Total Occupancy: 55

Bathrooms: One per each three or four person apartment

Co-Ed: Yes

Percentage of Men/Women: 41%/59%

Percentage of First-Year Students: 0%

Room Types: Standard

Special Features: Air Conditioned, Kitchenette with: small refrigerator, sink, microwave Large Living room including: TV hookup and cable availability, sofa, coffee table and other furniture provided, Adjacent parking lot.

New Apartments

Total Occupancy: 150

Bathrooms: Large bathroom in each apartment

Co-Ed: Yes

Percentage of Men/Women: 50%/50%

Percentage of First-Year Students: 0%

Room Types: Standard

Special Features: Air Conditioned, Kitchenette with: small refrigerator, sink, stovetop burners. Large Living room in-

cluding: TV hookup and cable availability, sofa, coffee table and other furniture provided, adjacent parking lot.

Taft Cottages

Total Occupancy: 48

Bathrooms: One per each four person apartment

Co-Ed: Yes

Percentage of Men/Women: 34%/66%

Percentage of First-Year Students: 0%

Room Types: Standard

Special Features: Air Conditioned, Kitchenette with: small refrigerator, sink, microwave Large Living room including: TV hookup and cable availability, sofa, coffee table and other furniture provided, large windows, laundry facility in building A Window seats on second floor, cathedral ceilings on third floor.

Number of Dormitories:

13

Undergrads on Campus:

99%

Percentage of Students in Singles:

31%

Percentage of Students in Doubles:
55%

Percentage of Students in Triples/Suites:
3%

Percentage of Students in Apartments:
11%

Bed Type
36"x 76"

Cleaning Service?
Residence Hall bathrooms are cleaned daily, apartment bathrooms are cleaned once a week.

Students Speak Out On...
Campus Housing

"I've never been unhappy with anywhere I've lived at Kenyon. Every year, I feel like I've always been given a good room, and I think that for the most part all of the dorms are pretty nice. Obviously, some are nicer than others, but we don't have any real high rises, we have one high rise building on campus, but I think we are lucky that the majority of our dorms are not more than two stories high."

Q "The lack of off-campus housing enhances the sense of community. **I love living on campus.**"

Q "There is a range of on-campus housing. We have a few beautiful dorms, mostly doubles and triples, with a few singles, which are populated primarily by frat boys and party kids. **The freshmen housing is grim, but fosters a real sense of community.** By the time you get to be a junior and senior, it's possible to get an on-campus apartment, some of which are stunningly beautiful, and some of which are pretty ramshackle; we get by."

Q "No matter how nice your dorm is, it will feel like a dungeon by the end of the first month. There are many methods to counteract this. For instance, do your homework somewhere else. **Walk outside and, in the typical freshman fashion, gawk at the image of Pierce Tower against the stars.** To be content on this campus, you need to appreciate quiet beauty, walking through fields, etc. It helps to have a friend with a car."

Q "Most of the on-campus housing offered is clean and comfortable, **but there aren't nearly enough singles on campus.** A small, close community like Kenyon can be a wonderful place to spend four years, but in order to thrive in such a tight-knit environment, personal space is so important. Especially for juniors and seniors, who are really becoming adults, being forced to live with roommates for four years can be stifling."

Q "The rooms in the freshman quad are huge. These are some of the biggest I've been in anywhere, and I did a lot of college touring. **The dorms are all really nice** if you want to make them nice. The windows are big, and there's lots of wall space to decorate and such."

Q "Housing is okay. Bexley's, New Apartments, and Aclands, which are **upper-class housing, are a lot nicer** than the dorms, which are very antiquated."

Q "Some at Kenyon feel that some of the money spent on the FRA should have gone to building new dorms. While there are some nice dorms that might score an eight out of ten, **far too many students, especially sophomores, feel there is definite room for improvemen**t."

Q "If you wanted to get an accurate view of Kenyon's dorms, you need only look at the ones designated for freshmen. First there are Norton and Lewis, which are known as the historics. **Externally beautiful with spacious rooms, these dorms are generally the preferred ones**, despite the absence of amenities such as air conditioning and carpeting, which are featured in McBride and Mather."

Q "Caples, an upper-class dorm, is a nine-story pencil, and is generally considered **the least desirable dorm on campus.**"

The College Prowler Take On...
Campus Housing

In the interests of maintaining a community, Kenyon maintains a strict residential campus. Students, with a few exceptions, live on campus all four years, and in these times, the dorms function as centers of non-academic student life. Kenyon housing can be evenly divided into two categories—dorms and apartments. Freshmen all live in dorms, and they live in the same area of campus. Lewis, Norton and Gund make up the freshmen quad. These dorms are not carpeted or air-conditioned, but the rooms are large and the architecture resembles that of the historic buildings of South campus. Across the street from those buildings are the two other frosh dorms, Mather and McBride. These rooms are slightly smaller, but they are air-conditioned, and their separation fosters its own tight-nit community. There are a fair number of available singles in these dorms and a doctor's note is the surest way to get one.

The other options for housing at Kenyon are in one of the many on-campus apartments. There are three, four and six person apartments available. Many juniors and seniors live the apartment life. Some of the most desirable of the upperclass apartments are the Bexley's, where every inhabitant gets a single. Farr hall, which is in the exact center of campus—above the bookstore—features bathrooms and kitchens. South campus has its Taft Cottages, which actually look like very nice real-world apartments, and give the Bexley's a run for their money. They are the newest buildings on campus, unlike the "New" Apartments, which have been around for decades. The last apartment option is the Aclands. They are located in the middle of campus, and have their own parking, but are slightly dilapidated. The enormous common rooms enhance the overall appeal, but also lend themselves to a great many parties. These are fun for the owner of the apartment, but can be less fun for the surrounding neighbors.

The College Prowler™ Grade on

Campus Housing: B-

A high Campus Housing grade indicates that dorms are clean, well-maintained, and spacious. Other determining factors include variety of dorms, proximity to classes, and social atmosphere.

Off-Campus Housing

The Lowdown On...
Off-Campus Housing

Undergrads in Off-Campus Housing:
15

Best Time to Look for a Place:
There is primarily no off-campus housing because of school policy.

Students Speak Out On...
Off-Campus Housing

"I absolutely love the fact that there is barely any off-campus housing. It unifies the campus. I visited a larger university in Atlanta, and most sophomores lived off-campus and had to commute to class. Part of Kenyon's magic is walking by the same people on the Middle Path and eventually stopping and saying 'Hey, I see you all the time. What's your name?' And you make a friend. That wouldn't happen if people lived off-campus."

Q "**There are a lot of apartments around, but** finding a cheap one near campus can be a little tricky. If you want one, you can find one without too many problems; you just have to look around. A lot of juniors and seniors eventually move off campus to avoid the guest policy and get cable (that's one thing that really sucks about BU dorms — no cable TV)."

Q "**Off-campus housing is decidedly inconvenient**, since almost all activities are based on campus."

Q "**Living off-campus is usually a moot point because several apartment complexes** (of varying, though generally good quality) exist on campus, and for most seniors, it is possible to get one of these apartments through the housing lottery."

Q "**An increasingly popular trend for those left in the cold by the lottery,** is to find an underclassmen willing to pay both shares in a double in exchange for the senior living in a vacancy in an off-campus apartment."

The College Prowler Take On...
Off-Campus Housing

We don't have very many students that live off campus. There are fifteen people that live off campus, but they underwent the very selective application process. Kenyon strongly believes in its community, and as a result everyone lives together on campus. The only exceptions to this stringent rule are a slightly larger percentage of students who live in apartments that are designated "off-campus" by about twenty yards. The "Milk Carton" apartments are visible from the dining hall and throw a lot of parties in warm weather. Each milk carton seems to correspond to a specific frat, sport or visible social clique, so you can usually determine the crowd of a party just by knowing the apartment number. The "Pizza Hut" apartments are slightly farther away, and look like low-rise city project housing.

One other thing to know about these apartments is that nobody is living there by school permission, so students can be very creative in how they live there. The most popular trick is to apply for a double on campus and not live in it. That way, you get your apartment and the other person gets a double single. This is a fairly common practice, and results in a lot of students with double singles.

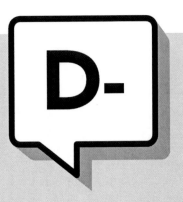

The College Prowler™ Grade on

Off-Campus Housing: D-

A high grade in Off-Campus Housing indicates that apartments are of high quality, close to campus, affordable, and easy to secure.

Diversity

The Lowdown On...
Diversity

American Indian:
1 = .062%

Asian or Pacific Islander:
50 = 3.14%

African American:
46 = 2.89%

Hispanic:
37 = 2.32%

White:
1,394 = 87.78%

International:
44 = 2.59%

Unknown:
60 =3.77%

Out of State:
1266 = 74.55%

Political Activity

Many Kenyon students have outspoken political beliefs, and all student e-mails (allstus) are a popular forum for political debate. Rallies or demonstrations are few and far between, but they do occur.

Gay Tolerance

Most students at Kenyon are fairly tolerant in terms of homosexuality. There have been isolated incidents of insensitivity, but they do not represent the opinion of the campus as a whole. The school recently opened a unity house to serve as a community center and safe space for the GLBTQQA community.

Most Popular Religions

The school was founded as Episcopalian, and although the tie between Kenyon and church is almost non-existent, Christians are still the biggest group on campus; however, there seems to be adequate Jewish representation as well.

Economic Status

The typical Kenyon is the product of a suburban upbringing and a private school, thus many of the students come from upper-middle-class backgrounds, but there are plenty of exceptions to the rule.

Minority Clubs

Adelante, ALSO (Allied Sexual Orientation), ASIA (Asian students for international awareness), ISAK (International Students at Kenyon).

Students Speak Out On...
Diversity

"Is its lack at Kenyon noticeable?—Yes. Kenyon's lack of diversity is noticeable, but not as bad as one would think. When I applied to schools, diversity was something I looked at mainly because it seems pompous and borderline discriminatory not to look, but when it boils down to it, it's not that big of a deal."

Q "Kenyon's diversity is not lacking in any means. **Everyone is so different.** it's incredible. If you base diversity on skin color, yes, Kenyon lacks diversity in race, but in every other aspect, religion, lifestyle, economic background, and life experiences, each person is fascinating."

Q "I would say that at Kenyon, you have a very diverse group of upper-middle-class, white students. Kenyon has a fairly large amount of international students, but there aren't a lot of African American students that are attracted to Kenyon. **I think that the admissions office works very hard to find African-American applicants**, but it hasn't really gotten to the point where Kenyon is as diverse as it could be. Maybe that has to do with its location being in Ohio."

Q "It takes a certain type of student to go to college in really what is the middle of nowhere in Ohio. **It is a great school and there is a lot that it offers,** but for a lot of people they really are forced to make their own fun during the week and weekends, therefore you have a lot of very independently minded students."

Q "There's a lack of diversity, and it is noticeable, but Kenyon does have the most diverse group of upper middle class white students. Also, **Kenyon is working on improving racial diversity as well as sexual diversity**."

Q "There are people literally from all over the world and all 50 states. **There is every religion** and ethnic group you could imagine."

Q "I have definitely met a lot of people from different states and different countries. There are also a lot of religions on campus and **a lot of religious activities**, so if you are religious at all or just want to meet people in the same religion, there are a lot of opportunities for that."

Q "I came from an almost all-white high school, and it was great to be surrounded by all ethnicities and backgrounds. It is such a **wonderful cultural experience**."

Q "Culturally, Kenyon College is very diverse. Overseas, it is an extremely popular university to attend, so it **attracts students from many continents** and countries around the world. Chances are, you will have several international students in every class, which provides for a much more dynamic and culturally-relevant discussion of the subjects."

The College Prowler Take On...
Diversity

Kenyon is a small, expensive school in a remote location, and as a result attracts a very specific type of student. A portrait of a typical Kenyon student is white and fairly affluent. While the school is having some success in racially diversifying the campus, racial minorities are still minor. Efforts to add some socio-economic diversity seem to have faired slightly better, bringing a different perspective to the school.

Diversity expands to looking at other students' backgrounds, and in that respect, Kenyon is diverse. If ones definition of diversity is based on skin color, then Kenyon is not very diverse. When looking at diversity one has to look beyond skin color or ethnic background and look at things such as religion, economic background and where students are from geographically. There are quite a bit of students who are not only from different states in the United States, but also are from different countries. A quarter of Kenyon students are from Ohio, but geographic diversity is increasing. The school is gaining a better reputation on the coast, attracting many from both New York and California. Washington D.C. and Maryland both have spectacular showings at Kenyon, and non-Ohio Midwesterners, most notably from the Chicago area, are increasing their numbers.

The College Prowler™ Grade on
Diversity: D+

A high grade in Diversity indicates that ethnic minorities and international students have a notable presence on campus and that students of different economic backgrounds, religious beliefs, and sexual preferences are well-represented.

Guys & Girls

The Lowdown On...
Guys & Girls

Men Undergrads:
769

Women Undergrads:
821

Birth Control Available?
Yes

Social Scene:
There are two distinct breeds of parties on campus. The first is the dimly lit, tightly packed, multi-keg-booty-dancing and singing-along-to-classic-rock party. These usually take place in dorm lounges or fraternity lodges, and are a great way to simply cut loose on a weekend night. There beer lines are long, however, and the atmosphere is not very conducive to actual conversation, and students often become disillusioned with

the whole scene as they get older. These parties are most fun if you either are really drunk or very fond of dancing. Those who don't find either criteria appealing usually stick to the apartment scene.

Juniors and seniors living in college apartments will often throw smaller parties. An apartment party can run the gamut from several friends hanging out to floor-sagging ragers, but usually they falls somewhere in the middle. There are several distinct advantages to this scene. The first is that you are actually able to talk to someone without screaming in his or her ear. It is often easier to find a drink in these situations, and they often go on much later than the registered lounge parties, which are broken up at two o'clock by security.

Every year, Kenyon pays for two school-wide parties. The first, Philanders Phling, happens in February and is designed to help students get through the long, Ohio winter. It is a formal even, thrown in Pierce Hall, and seemingly the entire campus shows up, drunk and in their Sunday best. While it can be a blast, many first-years complain that it is reminiscent of prom, where the enormous buildup of the event leads to disappointment upon arrival. Also like prom, many students miss it by getting too drunk too soon, so caution is advised in that area.

The second of these parties, Summer Sendoff, is thrown in May, on the last weekend before finals. The drinking starts early in the morning and continues throughout the day at many informal barbeques and open rooms. The day is capped by a concert from a fairly famous band, and the drinking continues as long as the students can keep their eyes open, an ability usually lost around midnight. For many, Summer Sendoff is the highlight of the year.

Hookups or Relationships?
Kenyon's location pretty much narrows the dating options down to "meet you in the cafeteria" and "let's take a walk," so people here are usually either just hooking up or practically married. Kenyon's incestuously small enrollment leaves little room for middle ground.

Best Place to Meet Guys/Girls:

At the beginning of freshman year, much of the coupling happens within halls. Dorms are the first fully constructed social unit a freshman encounters, and as a result many decide to conduct their romantic affairs in-house. "Dorm-cest" usually leads down one of two roads. Some people graduate with boyfriends/girlfriends they've had since swimming pre-season four years prior, and some realize that the incredibly short walk-of-shame isn't worth seeing your hook-up every morning when you're brushing your teeth.

After that, Kenyon is so small and personable that virtually any populated campus location can serve as a singles bar. The bookstore, the library, even the servery line are all perfectly viable locations to strike up a conversation with someone you've had your eye on. Striking up a conversation with a stranger is very easy to do. Comments on the class you have together or the length of the cafeteria line can easily lead to friendships, dates, and who-knows what else.

If you're the less patient type, immediate gratification can most easily be found at a frat party. Kenyon people are very friendly as it is, so putting 100 or so drunk ones in a room together, combined with low-lighting and booty music, can lead to a lot of interesting situations.

Did You Know?

Top Places to Find Hotties:
1. The Library (it's a bar without alcohol)
2. Frat parties (if that's your scene)
3. Denison University (sad but true)

Top Places to Hookup:

1. Mather Laundry room
2. Weaver Cottage
3. The Library Atrium
4. Someone else's room
5. The art barn

Dress Code

Looking around a Kenyon cafeteria, a newcomer would see a very confusing pastiche of styles. At a given table, you could see a girl wearing a J. Crew tank top talking to a guy in a full sweat suit who is sitting next to someone wearing a top hat and a cape.

Though it may seem confusing at first, Kenyon students dress habits can be broken up into three distinct cycles, no matter what their personal style is. The daytime mode of dress is typical collegiate casual. You will see people in classes or at lunch wearing sweatpants, t-shirts, fleeces and the like. This usually lasts until dinner time when the slightly more presentable clothes are put on to match the social scene in Pierce Dining Hall or Olin Library. This is the time when students put in immense amounts of effort to look like they got dressed effortlessly. The third style of dressing, party night, finds every social group dressed in their typical fashion, but more so. Preppy guys put on button ups and the hipsters find their favorite thrift store t-shirts. If necessary, a student could make it through their four years here without ever donning a tie or dress. There is the occasional semi-formal, usually thrown by the frats, but if you arrive late enough no one cares what you wear.

In general, the Kenyon rule seems to be "look decent." You don't walk around the bookstore at night in mesh shorts and a muscle shirt (though it happens), but if you put in a slight effort no one is going to call you a slob.

Students Speak Out On...
Guys & Girls

"Relationship wise, you find that there is no middle ground or very little middle ground. Some couples are very, very close and tight, almost married, to just occasional hook-ups, but you'll probably find that everywhere."

Q "People either get engaged or hook-up. There's nothing in between. **There are a lot of attractive people,** but most of them are engaged."

Q "It is about a half-and-half split between hookups, friends with benefits, and really intense relationships. **There's a good range of attractiveness on campus.**"

Q "Everyone is different, but I think that since you will be living with the same people for four years **some people are intimidated** by the fact of hooking up and having relationships early in their Kenyon career."

Q "For any teenage male, anything with two legs usually attracts attention. If physical beauty is your thing, yes, you'll find it at Kenyon as well as the true beauty of a person— their personality. **Girls dress really nicely, so I can't wait until spring and warm weather.**"

Q "In terms of relationships on campus, I'd say the campus is pretty divided. **There are those who want random hook-ups,** but as time goes on, often you hear stories from the same individuals over and over, and realize it's more of a 'hook-up circle.' The people who want relationships are often harder to find, but are there. In terms of how 'hot' the student body is, there are 'hot' people, and then there are those who don't classify people as hot or not. **Whichever you are, you'll find your clique, and if it's hot people you want,** you'll find them. It will help if you are a guy, because the guy/girl ratio favors you."

Q "**Most people I know have found long-term relation-ships**, but the general consensus on whether guys and girls are hot seems to be a resounding no on both ac-counts."

Q "Most of the people in my dorm go for casual hook ups, but then **we're the 'party' freshman dorm**, so I don't know how universal that is."

Q "**Kenyon is a very good looking campus with all sorts of types**—it just depends on what you're looking for. But yes, as a girl, for the most part, the guys are definitely more attractive than guys I've seen at other schools."

The College Prowler Take On...
Guys & Girls

After a little time at Kenyon, you will become very familiar with a little thing called "the Kenyon goggles." This is a phenomenon that allows average looking men and women to be thought of as extremely hot by the rest of the student body. Why? For a school once rated as one the country's most promiscuous, our general student body is not always easy on the eye. There are a great many cuties, but genuine hotties run far and few between. As a result, ordinary and slightly-above-average looking people find it extremely easy to find dates and hookups, and even the most unlikely student can find someone they really like. The good news is that we are improving. While many still feel that Kenyon guys are better looking than Kenyon girls, each incoming class brings in its notable additions, and the general looks of things are improving.

Once you decide exactly who you have your eye on, you may discover that someone you know has already done, dated, and/or dumped this person. It is not that we are overly promiscuous, but dating tends to happen within certain social circles. Certain guys have been known to tear through particular female groups of friends and vice versa. There is also the strong incestuous vibe that comes with being in such a close community. Everyone knows everybody else's business and it hard to meet someone with a clean slate if you have any kind of history on campus. For that reason, there is not a whole lot of dating. There is a lot of hooking up, and a lot of serious couples, but there are not a whole lot of people in the process of getting to know each other. If both parties go to Kenyon, chances are they already know each other.

The College Prowler™ Grade on

Guys: B-

A high grade for Guys indicates that the male population on campus is attractive, smart, friendly, and engaging, and that the school has a decent ratio of guys to girls.

The College Prowler™ Grade on

Girls: C+

A high grade for Girls not only implies that the women on campus are attractive, smart, friendly, and engaging, but also that there is a fair ratio of girls to guys.

Athletics

The Lowdown On...
Athletics

Athletic Division:
NCAA Division III

Conference:
NCAC

Men's Varsity Sports:
Baseball
Basketball
Cross Country
Golf
Indoor Track
Lacrosse

Outdoor Track
Soccer
Swimming
Tennis

Women's Varsity Sports:
Basketball
Cross Country
Field Hockey
Indoor Track
Lacrosse
Outdoor Track

→

Soccer
Swimming
Tennis

Intramurals:
Soccer
Football
Basketball

Club Sports:
Men's Rugby
Women's Rugby
Ice Hockey
Ultimate Frisbee

Athletic Fields
McBride Feld
Mavec Field
McCloskey Field

School Mascot
Lords and Ladies

Getting Tickets
Tickets are free to students, and some games at McBride Field may be $1

Most Popular Sports
Lacrosse, Basketball

Overlooked Teams
Swimming
Cross Country
Tennis

Best Place to Take a Walk

The Kokosing Gap trail is an Ohio landmark that begins in Gambier

Gyms/Facilities

Ernst Center

The Ernst Center is the main Athletic Facility on campus. It has a nice gym and a pool, which although primarily used for varsity teams also is available at certain times for non- athletes. As Kenyon is in a transition period in terms of facilities, the majority of the weights have been crammed into a squash court in Ernst, and while the space is small, the equipment is generally in decent condition.

The Temporary Facility

The Temp is essentially a practice gym for many of the out of season teams. It has a large surface that can be two basketball courts. It also has a small weight area with free weights and a few machines.

"**Kenyon is definitely not a jock school. The typical Kenyon student is very intellectual, very interested in classes; a lot of people talk about their classes outside of the classroom. Everyone seems to think pretty strongly about everything that goes on at Kenyon. They are very conscious of the community around them, and athletics are important, but there is definitely not that much of an emphasis put on them.**"

Q "Kenyon is definitely not a jock school, but almost everyone participates in athletics of some sort. Academics are the first priority and then extracurricular activities. The community isn't as involved with our sports as they may be in Miami, Florida. **Swimming is definitely our strength in the athletic realm,** but Kenyon surprisingly has many teams that are very competitive in their division. Cross Country is probably the most overlooked sport on campus."

Q "Football's not too big here. **IM sports are a popular way to have fun** and carry-on playing sports if you're not too serious about them."

Q "We excel at geeky, patrician sports like swimming, and are laughably bad at jock sports like football. With that said, **a huge number of people here are active and athletic without being jocks.** Intramural sports are popular and a lot of fun."

Q "As to the athletic scene, **intramural women's rugby is decidedly the optimal sport on campus.** Anyone can play; the captains are willing to teach you. There are no coaches, just other girls. It's a great way to stay in shape, get out aggression, and feel unconventional. It also guarantees you a safe and song-filled social life—C'mon now!"

Q "I feel like a majority of the students do play sports here, but I don't get the sense that it's a jock school. **And if you don't play a sport, you're definitely not looked down upon.**"

Q "Kenyon is not a jock school, although I see it rapidly getting there, with the addition of FRA. At the same time, we needed a new facility desperately, and this will most definitely attract student athletes. **I don't want to see it move towards a division in the student body as a XC runner.** I enjoy the fact that I can be a student, a singer, a writer and an athlete without feeling the need to restrict myself. Sports are moderately important to students, and not so to the community, with the exception of swimming, which I wouldn't consider a jock sport. I think swimming and football get the most attention, for opposite reasons. In addition, the 'game-oriented' sports such as soccer and field hockey get the most attention. Due to the nature of the sport, XC is overlooked, and golf is non-existent, but understandably so."

Q "In terms of quantity of sports, **Kenyon matches up well with any other Division III, liberal-arts school.** Quality however, is at best, another matter entirely. While there are some successful programs, the majority of Kenyon teams are mediocre."

Q "The two highest profile sports are football and men's basketball. **Football, which has heightened importance because of Kenyon's location in Ohio**, is 5-25 the last three years, and men's basketball, three coaches in four years, regularly only draw 300-400 people to a weekend game. Those numbers put us near the bottom of our conference."

Q "IM sports are a presence at Kenyon drawing perhaps an additional twenty percent of students to athletics **primarily through soccer, football, and basketball leagues.**"

The College Prowler Take On...
Athletics

While there is a football team at Kenyon, it is not exactly a campus benchmark. Neither are most sports for Kenyon students. This is not a jock school. On a campus comprised of many talented writers, artists, and scientists, sports simply do not occupy a significant spot on the Kenyon student's agenda. Football games are perhaps the most attended sport, followed closely by basketball games in the winter, however, a Saturday afternoon game will draw only a couple hundred students. The non-athletic student body is also not enticed by the reputation of Kenyon sports, especially in the recent past. The men's basketball team is on its third coach in four years. The football team has won just five games in the past three seasons. After a loss against perennial bottom-feeder Oberlin, an even less athletically minded school then Kenyon, we received a write up on Espn.com that ended with the phrase, "which raises the question, how bad is Kenyon?" With the hiring of a coach who specializes in reviving nearly-dead programs, Kenyon is hoping to turn the football team around. The exception that laps the rule, quite literally, are the swim Lords and Ladies. Kenyon's swimming teams have built themselves into a powerhouse for nearly the last quarter century. They have reined over Division III and regularly recruit Division I-caliber athletes. The men have captured the last twenty-five straight Division III National Championships, and the women have won twenty in twenty-one years. Kenyon has become nationally renowned as a school for "swimming and English." The thought that the swimmers will win has taken its place next to the English major being on the breadlines after graduation as a campus-wide assumption.

About 15-20 percent of the school tries to recapture their high school glory by playing in one of the IM leagues. Though these games don't draw huge audiences, the team members like to create rabid inter-league rivalries that will occasionally spill over into other realms of Kenyon life. Trash talk can spread to the dorms, cafeterias and email accounts until the rest of the campus will be forced to respond, even if it is to merely say "shut up."

C-

The College Prowler™ Grade on

Athletics: C-

A high grade in Athletics indicates that students have school spirit, that sports programs are respected, that games are well-attended, and that intramurals are a prominent part of student life.

Nightlife

The Lowdown On...
Nightlife

Club and Bar Prowler: Popular Nightlife Spots!

What to Do if You're Not 21:

Because of Kenyon's location, what to do under or over 21 is limited to mostly on-campus activities. There are always events being held, parties to attend, or sporting events to participate in or go see.

Favorite Drinking Games:

Beer Pong

Card Games

Never Have I Ever

Quarters

Power Hour

Roxanne

Frats:

See the Greek Section!

Students Speak Out On...
Nightlife

"There are a lot of options for nightlife at Kenyon—as many as you can expect at a small school. You hear very few complaints about there being things to do. A lot of people, if there isn't something to do, will create fun for themselves. I think that is one of the greatest skills you can learn coming out of Kenyon. You really won't have things arranged or planned for you. People are forced to become very independent and create fun for themselves, whatever that may be."

Q "**Fun parties usually get broken** up by a bored security force."

Q "You don't have to participate in the party scene, but it is hard to ignore. **There are all kinds of parties, though.** There are beer-soaked keg affairs, semi-formal invite soirees, and the more colorful affair—cross-dress debutante balls, mustache parties, short shorts parties, and sweaty, 80s post-punk disco dance happenings."

Q "The nightlife at Kenyon, if you like frat parties, is passable or so I've heard. If you enjoy hanging out with friends, it's nirvana. There is enough to do if you don't need fast paced big city life. **The Grille is sufficient, except for its distinct resemblance to a nasty basement.** I personally am for the abolition of fraternities on campus, so I can't really comment on frat parties."

Q "**I'm always busy with parties**, clubs, girls or whatever. We find stuff to do as teenagers."

Q "**There's enough to do if you're ready to go and find it.** There are always coffee houses with musicians on the weekends, along with movies that some people like to go to. And of course there are your frat parties, which are more like dances in the lounges, and then there are the nights where you just hang out with your friends in your dorm."

The College Prowler Take On...
Nightlife

The major party nights at Kenyon are Wednesday, Friday and Saturday, but if a person really wants to go out there is usually some small gathering to attend. Fraternities usually invite their friends and correspondent girls over for informal drinking some Mondays and Thursdays, and there are always people that will drink in their room with a couple friends. Most students who opt out of the big parties will either stay in or hang out in one of the upperclass apartments. These are again usually confined to groups of friends hanging out, but the larger size and relative lack of security in these area's makes them conducive to casual partying. One of the few things that Kenyon might have in common with OSU is our love for drinking games. Because Kenyon lacks a bar scene or student union, we use these games as a way to bond. Many close friendships have been given their start over a Beirut table. Security's recent crackdown on these games served more as a validation than a deterrent. All we have to do is play a little more quietly.

For those who actually are of age, the only place where you can utilize 21-year-old privilege is at "The Cove." You won't find The Cove listed anywhere on Kenyon's campus. It doesn't actually exist-by that name anyway. The Cove was formerly The Pirates' Cove. It was bought by Kenyon and re-opened two years ago as the Gambier Grille, although no one calls it that. Standard issue Grille by day, at night it turns into the only bar on campus, and the epicenter of 21 and above nightlife. Let me state for the record that it earns this mantle not because it's the students' choice—it's their lack of options. The bar itself is a windowless room with dark concrete walls, decorated only by random street signs and beer placards. It doesn't bug most students. "It's just where we go," one might say.

D+

The College Prowler™ Grade on
Nightlife: D+

A high grade in Nightlife indicates that there are many bars and clubs in the area that are easily accessible and affordable. Other determining factors include the number of options for the under-21 crowd and the prevalence of house parties.

Greek Life

The Lowdown On...
Greek Life

Number of Fraternities:
8

Number of Sororities:
4

Percent of Undergrad Men in Fraternities:
28%

Percent of Undergrad Women in Sororities:
10%

Fraternities on Campus:
Alpha Delta Phi
Beta Theta Pi
Brothers United
Delta Kappa Epsilon
Delta Phi
Delta Tau Delta
Phi Kappa Sigma
Psi Upsilon

Sororities on Campus:
Epsilon Delta Mu
Nia
Theta Delta Phi
Zeta Alpha Pi

Other Greek Organizations
Greek Council, Archon Society, Peeps O'Kenyon

Students Speak Out On...
Greek Life

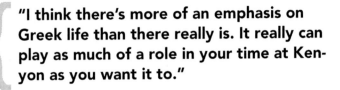

"I think there's more of an emphasis on Greek life than there really is. It really can play as much of a role in your time at Kenyon as you want it to."

Q "Greek life is not what it is on bigger campuses. Most of the big parties are thrown by frats, and that seems to be their primary contribution to campus life apart from the occasional blood drive or fundraiser. **The only real tension between Greeks and independents comes when housing rears its ugly head.** Fraternities do get a sort of housing advantage in campus residences, but it wouldn't be a problem if good housing weren't already in such short supply."

Q "**They exist to throw parties, take up tables in the dining hall, make dirty jokes, and gawk at girls.** The Greeks also screw up the housing lottery, make freshmen pledges puke, and sing songs about their fraternity. Come to think of it, I'm sure glad we have them on campus."

Q "It's definitely there, but not overwhelming at all. **It's also not Greek life as you would think of when you think of Animal House.** There's definitely always alcohol served, but I've felt that it's not the overwhelming facet of a frat party."

Q "The admissions office downplays the prevalence of Greek life on campus. Most parties on Wednesdays, Fridays and Saturdays are Greek-sponsored. However, **there are many alternatives**—coffeehouses, concerts, etc. Fewer people take advantage of these, but they are usually really amazing, and I haven't regretted going to any of them."

Q "**Fraternities do not live in houses**, but rather have sections of the dorms at one end of campus—although, their allotted housing is among the most desired."

Q "One's social life is **not defined by their affiliation**, or non-affiliation, with a certain fraternity."

Q "When my class came in, half of the males pledged; however, the average is closer to one third. In recent years **that number has dropped because of housing restrictions** placed on sophomores in fraternities.'"

Q "**Sororities play less of a role on campus because there are fewer of them (four as opposed eight fraternities),** and they lack the housing and lounges that fraternities have. About 15 percent of the most recent class of females are active in sororities."

Q "Even for fraternity-run parties, while there is an invite list sent out, **most anybody who comes down will be let in.** Fraternities at Kenyon are not exclusive."

The College Prowler Take On...
Greek Life

Admissions would be hard-pressed to admit this fact, but the Kenyon social scene is still largely dominated by the Greek system. Greeks have the most money and biggest lounges and lodges, and as a result they are able to throw the biggest parties attracting the largest numbers of people. In many other ways, the Kenyon Greek scene is anything but typical. Unlike bigger universities, a Kenyon student can completely decide to stay out of the Greek system while still enjoying access to Greek parties and the company of their Greek friends. Kenyon is such a close-knit school that fraternities and sororities serve more as clubs than exclusive societies. There are only eight fraternities and four sororities on campus. Since there would be no sense confining their parties just to members, most Greek bashes are open to anyone who would like to come. Invitations are put in people's rooms, but that serves mostly as a way to get the word out.

The rush system also works in a very unique way. First semester, fraternities do not throw any rush events. During this time, frats do everything they can do to get unofficially noticed. There are many parties aimed at freshman, and individual members also scout prospective pledges. By the time January rolls around, most fraternities have a good idea of who will at least be rushing, but there are always some surprises when it comes time to pledge. The advantage of having a Greek-free life first semester is that students build their own friends without the crutch of fraternities or sororities. This way, they always remain connected to the larger college community.

B-

The College Prowler™ Grade on
Greek Life: B-

A high grade in Greek Life indicates that sororities and fraternities are not only present, but also active on campus. Other determining factors include the variety of houses available and the respect the Greek community receives from the rest of the campus.

Drug Scene

The Lowdown On...
Drug Scene

Most Prevalent Drugs on Campus:
Alcohol, Marijuana, Ritalin, Aderall, Cocaine

Liquor-Related Referrals:
3

Liquor-Related Arrests:
0

Drug-Related Referrals:
0

Drug-Related Arrests:
0

Drug Counseling Programs
Responsible Choices

Students Speak Out On...
Drug Scene

"Kenyon's drugs of choice are cheap beer and Camel Lights. There's a fair amount of pot kicking around, some hallucinogens, a spot of E here and there. It's not really a big scene at all."

Q "I'm not a drug user, but there are plenty of people who smoke marijuana. I'm sure that there are plenty of drugs, but if you don't have any interest in drugs, they might as well be non-existent. **There are plenty of stupid decisions people make,** but as long as you make the right decisions you shouldn't have a problem."

Q "Don't do drugs."

Q "There is more cocaine than I thought there would be. **I never expected it, but people say it's easier to find cocaine than marijuana.**"

Q "The drug scene has a presence if you are looking for it. Most people aren't blatantly smoking pot at parties. They go in small groups to someone's room or somewhere outside. **Marijuana is definitely the drug of choice here.** I've heard some people do harder drugs, but I haven't seen or heard about that yet. It is not obvious at all, if it exists."

Q "It is evident that pot has its place at Kenyon. **It is difficult to gauge the percentage of active smokers,** however it is strong enough that it necessitates acknowledgement, however, it is also very possible to avoid it entirely without shutting oneself off from campus activities."

Q "For those into harder drugs, the search is a little more difficult. **There is isolated use of cocaine and ecstasy.**"

Q "**Drugs are there for those who choose to indulge;** however, they do not impinge on the lives of those who would rather not part take."

The College Prowler Take On...
Drug Scene

Surprisingly, Kenyon's remote location and general affluence have not fostered any major hard drug scene. Drugs do not come looking for you, but if you want them, they are not hard to find. Pot is a popular drug, and it can fairly easily be found on campus, depending on the season and the standards of the buyer. Many students are casual smokers, but becoming a serious stoner would impede on one's drinking life, and no one at Kenyon wants that to happen.

Most of the other drugs done here are of the hippy variety. Mushrooms and acid come around from time-to-time, but any coke or ecstasy is kept on the down-low. Since these types of drugs are done behind closed doors, there is a very slim chance that you will have issues with an RA or the campus police unless you draw attention to yourself. Alcohol is a drug and the most widely used drug, but most people think of the hard stuff when it comes to drugs. The most prevalent drug use probably comes around finals time, when Ritalin and Adderall become two of the most sought after items on campus.

The College Prowler™ Grade on
Drug Scene: B

A high grade in the Drug Scene indicates that drugs are not a noticeable part of campus life; drug use is not visible, and no pressure to use them seems to exist.

Campus Strictness

The Lowdown On...
Campus Strictness

What Are You Most Likely to Get Caught Doing on Campus?

- underage drinking
- marijuana
- parking illegally
- candles in the dorms
- smoking indoors

Students Speak Out On...
Campus Strictness

"They are not strict, no matter whether you're talking about drinking, parking, academics, or just about anything. This is both a good and bad thing."

Q "**Legal policies are very strict,** as well as the academic policies."

Q "Security has **a hard line to walk** and balances it pretty well."

Q "Bringing kegs on campus requires registering them with security. **Security is a presence at the parties where the beer is distributed.** They check to make sure that no one underage is served."

Q "**Security will only bust someone when there is obvious evidence that they are drinking underage**—the same goes for the dorms. While security makes regular rounds to make sure college policies are being adhered to, they will rarely intercede unless there is clear cut evidence of a violation."

The College Prowler Take On...
Campus Strictness

There is an interesting yo-yo effect when it comes to campus strictness – some years the security will be lax, others they will be nearly omnipresent. It goes back and forth. The biggest role of security, or at least the most visible one, is monitoring parties. They make sure things are safe, and the festivities end at the right time, but mostly they lurk around and ensure that no freshmen are drinking. In the past, freshman would put down there beers when they got word of security and the worst that would happen was being forced to pour out their cup. Now it seems that anyone caught drinking underage gets written up, but no one knows how long this new regime is going to last.

The other complication with Kenyon security is that the Knox County sheriff exploits the lack of real distinction between Kenyon and Gambier. Students stepping onto street with open containers of alcohol can easily get written up by the sheriff, and he also hands out the most expensive parking tickets. But it's not like campus security goes out and looks to write people up. They will only take action if they are forced to, so don't draw attention to the fact that you have been drinking if you are underage, and you should be fine.

The College Prowler™ Grade on

Campus Strictness: C

A high Campus Strictness grade implies an overall lenient atmosphere; police and RAs are fairly tolerant, and the administration's rules are flexible.

Parking

The Lowdown On...
Parking

Approximate Parking Permit Cost
$100

Common Parking Tickets:
Parking in faculty parking:
Parking in non-spaces

Student Parking Lot?
Yes.

Freshman Allowed to Park?
Yes.

Did You Know?

Best Places to Find a Parking Spot
The Norton, Lewis, and Watson lots north, behind Manning south.

Good Luck Getting a Parking Spot Here!
Behind Leonard

Students Speak Out On...
Parking

"It is terrible parking, especially for under-classmen. You don't need a car, but it's nice to have a friend who has one."

Q **"There are far too many cars on this campus,** which makes it hard to park."

Q "**South lot** is the hardest place to park."

Q "Parking is not a problem if you don't mind a five-minute walk to the freshman lot. I need a car because I couldn't stay in Gambier for the entire year, and I don't like to depend on other people. **Don't let other people use you though,** but having a car is definitely a huge benefit."

Q "It's annoying. They make the freshman park really far away from the freshman dorms when there are perfectly good and open spaces right outside the door. **You don't need a car, but it's really nice to have one if you want to get off-campus,** and not just take the shuttle to Mt. Vernon. Chances are you'll definitely have more than one friend who has a car."

Q "Parking is aweful. At the same time, **I wouldn't want to see parking lots take over Kenyon's greenery, so I guess we have to deal with it.** Surprisingly, parking was easiest my sophomore year, when I lived in Mather. We had access to Bexleys and Caples lot and Bexley Hall, and I usually got a spot. Freshman year, prepare to hike, junior and senior year, good luck getting a spot at Leonard or Manning—you probably won't. You don't need a car, unless you have an off-campus job, but it is handy. However, enough people have cars (judging from the crowded parking lots) that one is not necessary."

Q "Many similarly small schools do not allow freshman to bring cars. **Kenyon places no such restrictions on its newcomers.** However, there is a built in deterrent as freshman are required to park on the South end of campus, which is at the opposite end from their dorms."

Q "Upper-classmen are given stickers (either North or South) based on their housing assignment. **About one-fourth to one-third of the students bring cars,** and there is a minor parking crunch, because while there are enough spaces to accommodate the drivers, good spaces (closest to the dorms or other popular locations) are hot commodities."

Q "**A wrinkle in the parking situation is that because the college and the Village of Gambier are literally intertwined,** student drivers are subject to both the school's parking regulations and those of Gambier. The spaces on the main roads are governed by the Gambier Sheriff."

The College Prowler Take On...
Parking

There are enough parking lots to hold all of the cars at Kenyon, but convenient parking spaces are a little more of a commodity. At a little over a mile long, Kenyon prides itself as a walking campus. The only real use for a car (unless you're very lazy) is for going to and from campus. For these reasons, convenient parking, next to dorms and academic buildings, is few and far between. For upperclassmen, there is a very small number of very coveted spaces around the historic dorms, but the majority of South dwellers have to park in south lot, which is a down a big hill and pretty far from anything. Those living north fair a little better, with access to both south lot and any of the several smaller north parking lots around the apartments.

Kenyon is unique among small schools in that freshman are allowed to bring cars, and are guaranteed a place to park them. The only problem is that freshmen, who all live North, are given permits only to park in the south lot. This spells a pretty big trek for drivers, and can become a big deterrent to getting behind the wheel at all. This year especially, Kenyon has felt a shortage of desirable parking spot. One attempt at compensation was to offer free vehicle registration to drivers willing to park at an even more out of the way new lot, but there were not a lot of eager takers on that one. The college has said it will address the issue of parking when it drafts its new campus master plan, but student's remains skeptical on this point.

B-

The College Prowler™ Grade on

Parking: B-

A high grade in this section indicates that parking is both available and affordable, and that parking enforcement isn't overly severe.

Transportation

The Lowdown On...
Transportation

Ways to Get Around Town

On Campus

Campus is so small that walking is the only practical way to get around.

Public Transportation

Mt. Vernon Shuttle

Car Rentals

Alamo, local: (412) 472-5060; national: (800) 327-9633, www.alamo.com

Avis, local: (412) 472-5200; national: (800) 831-2847, www.avis.com

Budget, local: (412) 472-5252; national: (800) 527-0700, www.budget.com

Dollar, local: (412) 472-5100; national: (800) 800-4000. www.dollar.com

Enterprise, local: (412) 472-3490; national: (800) 736-8222, www.enterprise.com

Hertz, local: (412) 472-5955; national: (800) 654-3131, www.hertz.com

National, local: (412) 472-5094; national: (800) 227-7368, www.nationalcar.com

→

Ways to Get Out of Town

Airlines Serving Columbus:

American Airlines, (800) 433-7300, www.americanairlines.com

Continental, (800) 523-3273, www.continental.com

Delta, (800) 221-1212, www.delta-air.com

Northwest, (800) 225-2525, www.nwa.com

Southwest, (800) 435-9792, www.southwest.com

TWA, (800) 221-2000, www.twa.com

United, (800) 241-6522, www.united.com

US Airways, (800) 428-4322, www.usairways.com

Airport: Columbus International Airport approximately seventy-five minutes from campus.

How to Get There:

Columbus Transportation (800) 476-3004

A Cab Ride to the Airport Costs:

$100

Greyhound

Columbus (614) 228-2266

111 E. Town St.

Columbus OH 43215

Amtrak
Greyhound

111 East Town St.

Columbus, OH 43215

Travel Agents

AAA Travel Agency

(614) 228-2811 142 E Town St.

Columbus, OH

All Travel Plus

(614) 784-8172 4408 Olentangy Blvd.

Columbus, OH

American Express Travel Rltd

(614) 442-7400 5151 Reed Rd # 100b

Columbus, OH

Students Speak Out On...
Transportation

"Columbus is ninety-minutes away, no fooling. However, with the number of cars floating around it is easy to get away as there are shuttles to Mt. Vernon. You rarely need to get off-campus for material reasons: most often it's psychological."

Q "I thought I'd want to get off-campus all the time, because I thought Gambier would be constraining, but I was completely wrong. When I do want to get off-campus, it is very easy. **The shuttle service goes to Mount Vernon pretty much all the time.** The shuttle driver is very flexible, and will take you almost anywhere. One time I was sick, and he took me right back to my dorm. All-campus e-mails make getting to Columbus, the airport, and other cities extremely easy. Chances are you can catch a ride to pretty much any major Midwestern city when you need to go."

Q "It's very easy to get off-campus if you have a car. I need to get off-this campus once a week, and remember there is a real world outside of our little town. **If you have a car that's one less worry because you can take care of yourself without the aid of another person.**"

Q "The public transportation within the Gambier Corporation limits consists of the mile-long footpath known as middle path, which stretches the length of the campus. **Kenyon's campus is small enough that virtually any spot is reachable with a fifteen-minute walk.**"

Q "In terms of public transportation out of Gambier, there is a shuttle that drops students off in different points in Mt.

Vernon. It runs hourly in the afternoons and evenings on Monday, Wednesday, Friday and Saturday. **It is no cost to students, and is a perfect way to escape the hill for a bit**, either for a meal, some shopping, or to see a movie."

Q **"There is also a shuttle that runs twice a month to Columbus**—for those who need a taste of the city."

The College Prowler Take On...
Transportation

As small as it is, you can easily get settled into the Kenyon lifestyle, and never feel the urge to leave the hill. Every necessity is right there for you, and it is easy to be lazy about getting in touch with the outside world. With that said, getting out of Kenyon once in a while can be a wonderful thing. Seeing tall buildings and unfamiliar people every so often can help you both relieve stress and appreciate Kenyon even more. While not everyone on campus has a car, almost everyone has a friend who does, so securing wheels usually isn't a problem with a little persistence.

If it's a true emergency, or no one around you is able to lend a car, the college maintains a shuttle service. Four times a week a bus goes into Mount Vernon and picks up the students later at specified times, and once a month the college sends one into Columbus. The only area where transportation really becomes an issue is going to and from the airport. An outside shuttle service provides rides at the beginning and end of major breaks, but the price is almost never worth it. Instead, students take advantage of the "allstu" e-mail function to seek and offer rides. Even in last minute desperation, these rides will never cost more than the airport shuttle.

The College Prowler™ Grade on
Transportation: C+

A high grade for Transportation indicates that campus buses, public buses, cabs, and rental cars are readily-available and affordable. Other determining factors include proximity to an airport and the necessity of transportation.

Weather

The Lowdown On...
Weather

Average Temperature

Fall:	62.6 °F
Winter:	21.5 °F
Spring:	53.8 °F
Summer:	72.3 °F

Average Precipitation

Fall:	2.69 in.
Winter:	2.90 in.
Spring:	3.74 in.
Summer:	5.25 in.

Students Speak Out On...
Weather

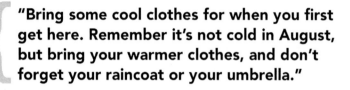

"Bring some cool clothes for when you first get here. Remember it's not cold in August, but bring your warmer clothes, and don't forget your raincoat or your umbrella."

Q "I made the mistake of bringing about ten tank tops, only one of which I used, and I used it as fabric for my quilt making class. Bring sweaters, sweaters, and more sweaters, along with a light, medium, and heavy jacket. I would strongly suggest getting a pair of UGGS boots. Don't bring just heavy clothes though. **The weather can be spastic, and you'll find yourself taking off your winter coat and putting on a short sleeve shirt and shorts all within the same day.**"

Q "Winter lasts from late October to late March or early April, and is characterized by unrelentingly gray skies, chilly winds, and a great deal of ice, but not much snow. It is pretty in a masochistically desolate sort of way. **Bring a warm coat, a scarf, earmuffs, ankle warmers, and warm boots.** However, fall and spring are so beautiful it is quite possible your heart will explode every time you walk outside."

Q "As for the seasons and your clothing—this is Ohio. I emphasize layers—the temperature fluctuates as much as ten degrees from one hour to the next. **Bring tank tops, t-shirts, long sleeve shirts and sweaters.** I guarantee you would be comfortable in one of each throughout the course of an average day. Bring mittens, a cute hat, boots, and an umbrella."

Q **"It's hot as hell when you get here in August and the beginning of September, but then it cools off** really nicely in September and early October. Winter seems to settle in around mid-October, and then you'll definitely need a warm winter coat, hat, gloves, scarf, the works."

Q **"The first few weeks in late August and early September are hot, with most days being at least seventy-five and some touching ninety.** The beginning of October marks the beginning of fall and temperatures cool to the sixties on most days. This is also the time when the leaves begin to turn and the rural campus is at the height of its beauty."

Q "With the exception of last year, which was inordinately snowy across the country, **Kenyon gets only a little snow each winter.**"

Q **"Dressing for success in this weather pattern requires a heavy jacket for the winter and sweaters in the colder months,** but that is book ended by an almost equal amount of time in shorts."

Q "Shortly before Thanksgiving break **the mercury dips to the 40s and 30s** and stays that way until the middle of February."

The College Prowler Take On...
Weather

Kenyon is in the Midwest: ergo, it has varying weather. This simple distinction often proves a big problem for southerners and Californians. The weather can be cold, but contrary to the belief of these warm-weather folks, it is always manageable. The first three weeks of school are very warm, and shorts and t-shirts gain exclusive popularity. Things begin to calm down a little bit toward the end of September, and the weather borders on perfect (if a little chilly) through mid-October. It is no coincidence that parents weekend falls near Halloween, when it is in the 50s and the leaves turn the campus into the most beautiful place in Ohio. Winter can be long and cold, but in the eyes of this Chicagoan I know it could be worse. There is snow, and it can grey outside, but the thermostat rarely drops below the thirties. The trade off for this dreariness is that springs starts up at full force after the break in March, and the genuine excitement on campus makes this one of the best times of year.

The way to be most comfortable in this climate is to be prepared for both the best weather conditions and the worst. As is listed above, have your shorts and t-shirts available for the earlier portion of the school year and also after April. Then you need long sleeved shirts, sweatshirts, and eventually hats, gloves and heavier jackets. The weather is bearable, but having the proper attire will make you the most comfortable.

The College Prowler™ Grade on
Weather: C+

A high Weather grade designates that temperatures are mild and rarely reach extremes, that the campus tends to be sunny rather than rainy, and that weather is fairly consistent rather than unpredictable.

Report Card Summary

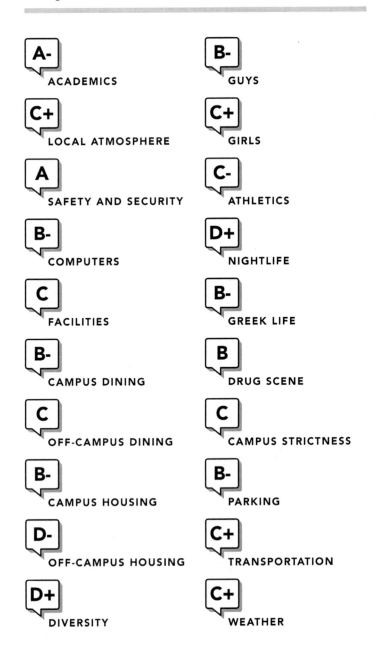

A- ACADEMICS

B- GUYS

C+ LOCAL ATMOSPHERE

C+ GIRLS

A SAFETY AND SECURITY

C- ATHLETICS

B- COMPUTERS

D+ NIGHTLIFE

C FACILITIES

B- GREEK LIFE

B- CAMPUS DINING

B DRUG SCENE

C OFF-CAMPUS DINING

C CAMPUS STRICTNESS

B- CAMPUS HOUSING

B- PARKING

D- OFF-CAMPUS HOUSING

C+ TRANSPORTATION

D+ DIVERSITY

C+ WEATHER

Overall Experience

Students Speak Out On...
Overall Experience

"The people are incredible, and have made my college experience wonderful. Kenyon is the perfect college for anyone who is serious about their studies and life in general. And of course you'll have an incredible time."

Q "Kenyon has poisoned me forever. **I desperately want to get on with my life and I never, ever want to leave.** This place is perfect and deeply dysfunctional. It is not in any way shape or form like real life and why should it be? It's college."

Q "Kenyon's a place where all the smart but quirky kids from high school came. **We like to learn for learning's sake, but we also like to have fun.** We play sports, we sing a cappella, we star-gaze and we play Ultimate Frisbee. There's definitely something to be said for 1,600 kids who want to spend four years in the middle of nowhere. We care about our education, but we really care about who we learn with. **The people here are awesome and if you take the time to get to know people, you'll always be presently surprised.** Cliché? Maybe, but I think it's true."

Q "**The main thing about Kenyon is the tradeoff between niceness and iconoclasticness.** Kenyon greets you with a warm welcome because everyone here is just so darn nice. But at the same time, since nearly everyone is nice to everyone else, the campus dynamic is just a little more flat than it could be. Speaking for me, the most important thing I was looking for was feeling at home. This is certainly true at Kenyon College, so for me, the tradeoff was definitely worthwhile."

Q "**I believe everyone at Kenyon has a 'Kenyon moment' that turns a switch and makes you truly appreciate Kenyon for all its good and bad aspects, because with everything considered, it is a one-of-a-kind and wonderful place.** As a disoriented freshman, I got lost trying to find the observatory for a Physics lab at 10 o'clock at night during the first week of school. I was somewhere near the athletic facilities, and I asked a lacrosse player if he knew where the observatory was. He said "no, but I have a car—we can go look for it." So at 10 p.m., after sports practice, a complete stranger drove me around for half hour looking for the observatory. It was a completely unnecessary yet benevolent gesture that I will always remember. It was one of my first impressions of Kenyon students, and one that they've certainly lived up to since."

Q "**If you had told me in the winter of my senior year of high school that I would be spending my college years in Gambier, Ohio, I would have questioned your sanity.** In truth, the three years have met the cliché, as the best of my life."

Q "The best part about the Kenyon experience is the feeling that you get from being there—a feeling that is not quantifiable and requires a first hand knowledge of the place to understand. **It is not merely one aspect of community, but rather the sum of many things that contribute to this feeling of comfort and warmth that Kenyon seems to exude.**"

The College Prowler Take On...
Overall Experience

Kenyon College is a small school in rural Ohio. There is no student union, and our "town" is one block long. The weather is unpredictable at best and half the dorms are said to be haunted. English, our most popular department, sends out its majors to work at supermarkets. However, you still wouldn't be able to ask any current student or alum, "Do you like Kenyon," without setting aside at least forty-five minutes for the answer. Kenyon casts a spell on everyone that passes through it: all the things that might initially make it sound unappealing are in the end what make the place so special. No one else will ever have a college experience quite like a Kenyon student. Everyone at Kenyon is there for the simple reason that they want to be. They have not come for the glamour of a big city; they have not come because of an Ivy-league name to drop at parties. They have chosen Kenyon in spite of all its deficiencies, or perhaps because of them. Our isolation simply means that there is nothing to distract us from learning and from each other.

Stuck up on this hill, we really have no choice but to reach out to one another. The reason no one locks their doors are the same reason that most "private" parties are open to the whole campus. As a freshman, you might make a new best friend because you're both wearing the same Yankee's cap. As a senior, you might make a new best friend because you've sat next to each other in the library for three weeks in a row. This unnaturally close community encourages and expects you to open up to all these non-strangers around you. The only times I ever wish I was somewhere else are the times when I'm away from Kenyon.

The Inside Scoop

The Lowdown On...
The Inside Scoop

Kenyon Slang:

Know the slang, know the school. The following is a list of things you really need to know before coming to Kenyon. The more of these words you know, the better off you'll be.

The Bullseyes: Two rooms with big round windows at the top of Old Kenyon that function as party spots for frats.

The Deuce: Large triple in Hanna used by the D-Phi's for Wednesday night parties.

Division: Wings of the historic dorms allotted to fraternity members.

The Pub: Philanders Pub, which serves pizza, and is located in the basement of Pierce.

Phling: Philanders Phling, a campus wide formal held every February in Pierce.

Gates of Hell: The two stone pillars that mark the entrance to South campus.

Beta Rock: A south-quad boulder held sacred by the

fraternity of Beta Theta Pi.

Allstu: An e-mail sent to the entire student body.

Milk Cartons: Off-campus houses that look like a milk cartons

Pizza Huts: Off-campus houses that look like pizza huts

The Hill: The general Kenyon area, which is set up on a hill

The Verne: Mount Vernon, our neighboring town

Hunan: Hunan Garden, a Chinese restaurant in Mount Vernon

The Grill: The Gambier Grill, the local bar and take-out restaurant

Middle Path: The path that runs the length of campus

Sexile: Temporarily kicking out your roommate to hook up with someone

DormCest/HallCest: Hooking up with someone else in your dorm or on your hall

The Atrium: The lobby of the library

The Horn: The Horn gallery, a performance space

The bank-box: A black-box theater located next to the post office

Philo: Philomathesian hall, on the second floor of ascension

Hot Rods: An all-night sandwich chain run out of gas-stations

New-aps: The new apartments

Shock your mama: An annual near-naked party thrown by the swimmers

The Deb-Ball: An annual drag ball

BFEC: The Brown Family Environmental Center

RFOC: Real Food on Campus: the new initiative by ARA

ARA: Aramark, the campus' food provider

Pink House: A pink house where the Phi-Kaps hold their parties

Things I Wish I Knew Before Coming to Kenyon

- No matter big your high school, 1,600 people is simply not a lot of people

- That a slightly skuzzy Chinese restaurant could become the be-all and end-all of weekend dining

- Writing is a necessary component of every conceivable academic subject

- Getting a bat out of a dorm room is more difficult than one would guess

- It is more difficult to find an open computer during finals than it is to pass the actual tests

- There truly are a lot of cornfields around here

- Ramen noodles can be eaten for breakfast, lunch, and dinner

- A good night's sleep is only for weekends and breaks

- Making out in public is not cool, even if you are drunk.

- In the eyes of upperclassmen, public use of a cell phone is synonymous with infectious disease.

- At a school this small, there is no such thing as secrets

Tips to Succeed at Kenyon

- Sucking up to profs will greatly help your chances of getting into a particular class
- Starting things off right does wonders for your GPA
- Don't pre-judge people in frats and sororities; most of them here are very nice.
- Watch yourself—it is easy to get a reputation at a school this small.
- Don't talk too loudly about people in the library; they or their best friend are probably sitting right behind you
- Make good friends, but keep your independence
- Rushing a fraternity or sorority does not make you obligated to join it.
- Getting off campus once in a while is good for your sanity
- Show up to classes, your professor will notice when you are not there.
- Don't let your drinking interfere with your life

Kenyon Urban Legends

- The basement of Sam Mather Hall contains the actual gate to hell
- When the church caught fire the flames burned downward
- Paul Newman '51 donated the $60 million for the new athletics facility
- Playboy once voted us the most promiscuous school in the country

School Spirit

Kenyon students are insanely proud of their college, but they rarely have occasion to express this. There is a great understood sense of accomplishment in going to Kenyon. We take pride in our high academic environment, and in the underlying trust and closeness of the Kenyon campus. Just because a person is not wearing white and purple does not mean they don't feel this. There is a quasi-rivalry with some of the shinier, but less academic schools in the area (Denison, Ohio Weslyan), but this is usually expressed only through snide comments and the occasional field hockey match. Probably the best indicator of school spirit is our annual Summer Sendoff, but the administration would never put it in our admissions booklet. Summer Sendoff is a day-long party that the school throws the day before the start of finals in May. This is the day when the entire campus comes together in the south quad to drink, barbeque, play games, and generally celebrate being at Kenyon.

Traditions

The Gates of Hell

The cornerstone of all Kenyon superstition is the two stone pillars, with a post in the middle, that mark the entrance to South campus. They were nicknamed both because they lead to all of the schools academic buildings, and because they are rumored to be the actual gates to hell. The traditions around them are endless. Some people refuse to walk through the gates at all. Some people never touch the post, some people always touch the post, some people urinate on the post. There are those that obey the laws of traffic, always going through the right hand "lane" and other that laugh at all these silly gates of hell traditions.

Freshmen Sing

Freshmen sing functions as the unveiling of the freshmen class to the rest of the school. On their third day of freshmen orientation, the entire freshman class lines up on the steps of Rosse Hall and belts out four Kenyon anthems to everyone standing below. Once they have completed these first four songs, and earned the respect of the rest of the school, we all join them for a final anthem, and they officially enter the Kenyon community. Freshmen Sing can also be used as a preliminary way to scout out the hot frosh.

Friday Afternoon Drinking Club

The Friday Afternoon Drinking Club, or FADC, is not at all school sponsored, but it still draws a fairly large crowd. Held in various locations around campus every Friday at 5 p.m., it has become a mainstay for campus drunks. If you want to want to kick off the weekend early, or at least come drunk to dinner, two dollars will get you all that you need at FADC.

Vendors on Middle Path

When the weather is nice, and sometimes when it's not, area merchants will set up stands on middle path and nearby Farr hall for student shoppers. Middle Path usually features Amish goods, such as scarves and baskets, as well as fresh local produce. Farr Hall, which is next to the bookstore, usually features slightly more commercial vendors, usually with a hippy twist. There is one man who frequently comes by to sell jewelry and incense, and occasionally used records.

Ghost Stories With Professor Shutt

Humanities Professor and campus legend Tim Shutt gathers students around a bonfire every Halloween for a terrifying trek through Kenyon's supposed haunted history. Going year-by-year and dorm-by-dorm, Shutt goes through every death and murder that has ever happened in Kenyon's history, and then tells how the victim presently haunts the school. Even those with the strongest of constitutions have been known to sleep with the lights on after this event.

Philanders Phling

Kenyon is a school with a lot of formal traditions, and a generally informal attitude toward dress and decorum. The formal and informal meet is at Philanders Phling, which is an annual winter formal thrown by the school. The ball is held every February, and is one of the most anticipated events of the year. It also is the only time that students really need to worry about looking like lords and ladies, but not about acting like them.

Summer Send-Off

The school throws summer send-off in early May as a sort of last hurrah before finals begin. The day starts with games and barbeques in the south quad, and ends with a concert by a fairly big name band. Students begin their drinking very early in the day, and often don't stop. This is the one day where a person can drink before lunch without getting dirty looks. Whether or not you partake in the debauchery, this is the only day where the entire campus appears truly united.

Frat Tables in Pierce

Pierce's great hall, the schools main dining room, can often serve as a microcosm of Kenyon social interaction. The tables are long enough for people to sit with their extended groups of friends, and fraternities have their own unofficially designated table. The Dekes sit near the entrance, Delts near the conveyer belt, and Betas sit on the heater. There is no real threat for crossing these undeclared boundaries, but a sign of true assimilation to Kenyon is learning which tables in Pierce belong to whom.

Finding a Job or Internship

The Lowdown On...
Finding a Job or Internship

The Lowdown

A liberal arts education like the one you receive at Kenyon teaches you how to think, the challenge afterward is getting a job to think for. The CDC is available to help in this endeavor.

Advice

Extern! Kenyon's externship program allows students to shadow someone in a field of interest for 3-5 days over a break. It is a great way to learn about a profession in which you might be interested in, and to network. Also talk to the CDC early and often in your senior year, they are very helpful for seniors.

Career Center Resources & Services

Career counseling, Graduate school counseling, Resume and cover letter workshops, and E-recruiting system.

Percent of Grads who enter job market :

Within 6 months after graduation: 95%

Within 1 year after graduation: 98%

Within 2 years after graduation: 99%

Firms That Most Frequent Hire Graduates:

3M, AG Edwards, Abbott Labs, ABC, ABN AMRO, Accenture, Adobe Systems, Aetna, Allstate, Am. Express Fin. Adv. , Am. Airlines, Am. Elec. Power, Amgen Inc. , AOL Brand Mktg. & Promotions, Aon Consulting, AT&T, Autodesk, Bank of America, Bank of Boston, Bank of NY, Bank One, Barclays Bank, Barnes & Noble, Battelle Memorial Inst. , Bear Stearns, Bloomberg, Blue Cross & Blue Shield, Boeing, Booz Allen Hamilton, Boston Globe, Bureau of Nat'l. Affairs, CB Richard Ellis, CBS, Chicago Public Sch. , Children's Hosp. Med. Ctr. , Christie's, Chubb & Son, Ciba Specialty Chemicals, Cincinnati Post, Cincinnati Public Sch. , Cisco, Citibank, Citicorp, Citigroup, City of NY, Cleveland Clinic, CNN, Coca-Cola, Columbus Acad. , Corning, Dayton Power & Light Co. , Deloitte & Touche, Deloitte Consulting, Delta, Deutsche Bank, Dow Chemical, DuPont, Eastman Kodak, Eaton Corp. , Eli Lilly, Episcopal Diocese & Churches, Ernst & Young, Estee Lauder, Exxon Mobil, Fannie Mae, FedEx, Fed. Res. Bank, Fidelity Investments, Fifth Third Bank, Fleet Bank, FleetBoston, Forbes Mag. , Ford Motor Co. , FOX, Gap, GE, Goldman Sachs, Guidant Corp. , H&R Block, Habitat for Humanity, Health Alliance Int¿l, Hewitt Associates, HBO, Houghton Mifflin, Humane Society of US, Huntington Nat¿l Bank, Hyatt Corp. , IBM, Intel, IRS, J. P. Morgan Chase, Janney Montgomery Scott, Johnson & Johnson, Jones, Day, Reavis, & Pogue, Kaiser Permanente, Kaplan, Key Corp, KPMG, LaSalle Bank, Legal Aid Soc. , Lehman Bros. , Lexis Nexis, Lockheed Martin, Lubrizol Corp. , Marsh USA Inc. , MA Gen. Hosp. , Mass. Mutual Life Ins. , Mayo Clinic, Mazda, McGraw Hill, McKesson, Mem. Sloan Kettering Cancer Ctr.

, Merck & Co. , Merrill Lynch, MetLife, Microsoft, Monsanto, Morgan Stanley, Morningstar, MTV, NASA, Nat'l. City Corp. , Nat'l. Geo. Soc. , Nationwide Ins. , Nat'l. Inst. of Health, NBC, NCR, NY Life Ins. , NY Times, Newsweek, Northern Trust Co. , NPR, Ogilvy & Mather, OH Attny. General, Oppenheimer Capital, Oxford U. Press, PBS, Peace Corps, Penton Publishing, Pfizer, Pharmacia, Philadelphia Inquirer, Pittsburgh Post-Gazette, Planned Parenthood, Porter, Wright, Morris, & Arthur LLP, Portland Public Sch. , Pricewaterhouse Coopers, Procter & Gamble, Progressive Insurance, Prudential Securities, Qwest Communications, RAND, Reader's Digest, Riverside Methodist Hosp. , Robert W. Baird, SAIC, Salomon Smith Barney, Scholastic Inc. , Siemens, Simon & Schuster, Social Security Admin. , St. Lukes Roosevelt Hosp. , St. Petersburg Times, St. Vincent's Med. Ctr. , Standard & Poor's, State Farm Ins. , States of AZ, CA, CO, HI, MD, OH, State Street Bank, Staten Island Acad. , Sun Microsystems, T. Rowe Price, TEK Systems, Texaco, Texas Instruments, The Nature Conservancy, The Princeton Review, TIAA-CREF, Time Warner, U. S. Air Force, U. S. Army, U. S. Coast Guard, U. S. Dept. of Commerce, U. S. Dept. of Defense, U. S. Dept. of Energy, U. S. Dept. of Justice, U. S. Dept. of State, U. S. Dept. of the Treasury, U. S. District Court, U. S. EPA, U. S. General Acctng. Office, U. S. Library of Congress, U. S. Marine Corps, U. S. Navy, U. S. Public Health Serv. , UBS Paine Webber, UBS Warburg, Unisys, United Air Lines, United Way, Veterans Admin. Med. Ctr. , Wachovia Securities, Washington Post, Wells Fargo, Westinghouse, Wired Mag. , World Bank, Xerox, YMCA

Alumni

The Lowdown On...
Alumni

Website:

http://www.kenyon.edu/
alumni.xml

Services Available
Keep email address at Kenyon for thirteen months after graduation

Alumni Publications
Kenyon Magazine

Major Alumni Events
We technically have homecoming, although it is not very popular. There is a reunion weekend for the intervals of five years the weekend after graduation. This is highly attended.

Did You Know?

Famous Kenyon Alumni:

Nick Bakay, 1981, actor, comedy writer, television producer

Doug Ballard, 1976, actor

Jim Bellows, 1944, journalist, editor

Jim Borgman, 1976, cartoonist ("Zits"), Cincinnati Enquirer political cartoonist, Pulitzer Prize winner

Francis Key Brooke, 1874, first bishop of Oklahoma (Episcopal)*

Ken Burgomaster, 1991, composer

Caleb Carr, 1977, writer (Alienist, Angel of Darkness)

Jay Cocks, 1964, film critic, Academy Award-nominated screenwriter

James Cox, 1960, physician, researcher, educator, M. D. Anderson Cancer Center

Meg Cranston, 1982, artist

Adam Davidson, 1986, director, Academy Award-winning filmmaker

Edwin Hamilton Davis, 1833, archaeologist (Ancient Monuments of the Mississippi Valley), medical educator, physician*

Carl Djerassi, 1943, writer, developer of the birth control pill

E. L. Doctorow, 1952, writer (Ragtime, Loon Lake), Pulitzer Prize winner

Rolla Dyer, 1907, developer of typhus vaccine, National Institutes of Health director*

Eric Gaskins, 1980, fashion designer

William Gass, 1947, writer (Omensetter's Luck, Tunnel), National Book Award winner

Graham Gund, 1963, architect

R. S. Harrison, 1953, retired chief executive, Baldwin Piano and Organ Co.

Rutherford B. Hayes, 1842, U.S. president*

Laura Hillenbrand, 1989, writer (Seabiscuit)

→

Murray Horwitz, 1970, director and chief operating officer, American Film Institute Silver Theatre and Cultural Center; commentator, National Public Radio

Allison Janney, 1982, Emmy-winning (West Wing) and Tony-nominated (A View from the Bridge) actor {She also stars in the new film Finding Nemo}

Robert Lowell, 1940, poet, Pulitzer Prize winner*

William Lowry, 1956, vice president, John D. and Catherine T. MacArthur Foundation

Robie Macauley, 1941, writer, editor (Kenyon Review, Playboy)*

Allison Mackie, 1982, actor

Wendy MacLeod, 1981, playwright (House of Yes), screenwriter

Don McNeill, 1940, U.S. Open tennis champion (singles, 1940)*

Paul Newman, 1949, Academy Award-winning actor, philanthropist

Kevin O'Donnell, 1947, former U.S. Peace Corps director

Oronhyatekha (Peter Martin), 1863, Mohawk Indian leader, physician, supreme chief ranger of Independent Order of Foresters*

Kris Osborn, 1999, CNN anchor, reporter

Olof Palme, 1948, prime minister of Sweden*

Kristina Peterson, 1973, former Simon & Schuster publishing executive

William Rehnquist, 1946, U.S. Supreme Court chief justice

Alphonse Rockwell, 1863, physician, electrotherapeutics pioneer*

Mark Rosenthal, 1973, president and chief operating officer, MTV Networks

Arthur "Chip" Sansom, 1973, cartoonist ("Born Loser")

Byers Shaw, 1972, physician, educator, liver-transplant pioneer

Ned Smyth, 1970, sculptor

John Snow, 1961, U.S. secretary of the treasury

Edwin M. Stanton, 1834, U.S. attorney general and secretary of war (Lincoln administration)*

James Storer, 1949, retired broadcasting executive

William Swing, 1958, bishop of California (Episcopal)

Geri Coleman Tucker, 1974, technology editor, USA Today

Bill Veeck, 1936, baseball innovator, major-league team owner*

Fred Waitzkin, 1965, writer (Searching for Bobby Fischer, Last Marlin)

Bill Watterson, 1980, cartoonist ("Calvin and Hobbes"), Lambda Book Award winner

Matthew Winkler, 1977, editor in chief, Bloomberg News

Jonathan Winters, 1950, actor, artist, comedian

Peter Woytuk, 1980, sculptor

James Wright, 1952, poet, Pulitzer Prize winner*

John Celivergos Zachos, 1840, pioneering educator, inventor (stenotype)*

Nancy Sydor Zafris, 1976, writer,

Flannery O'Connor Prize-winner

Student Organizations

ARSE (Arts-Related Student Entity): We promote and publicize opportunities for art-making and art appreciation, especially targeting campus and area opportunities like gallery openings, talks, etc., which we either plan or arrange transportation.

Horn Gallery for the Arts: All-student organizations that provides gallery space on a year round basis for the students. Art, music, and other performances occur at coffeehouse events that are held once a week.

Adelante: Adelante shall serve as an organization aimed at helping Hispanic/Latino students adjust to Kenyon's culture. ADELANTE's main objective is supporting Hispanic/Latino students and providing a sense of community on campus. The organization also spreads an awareness of Hispanic/Latino cultures. This will be achieved through lectures, films, and other social/educational activities.

ALSO (Allied Sexual Orientation): ALSO is a proactive group of committed leaders teaching and supporting the Kenyon Community on issues relevant to the queer experience.

ASIA (Asian Students for International Awareness):

The purpose of ASIA is to promote the sharing of Asian cultural experiences among all students on campus in the interest of multiculturalism.

BSU (Black Student Union): To offer support to Black students at Kenyon to preserve and affirm the cultures of its members. The BSU aims to raise the consciousness of the Kenyon community through formal and informal events.

Capoeira Club: The objective of the Kenyon Capoeira Club is to promote the Brazilian Martial Art/dance Capoeira among the College population. This will be done through member's participation in practicing the movements and learning about the music of the art, as well as through increased self-awareness and confidence in the participants. It offers physical and mental tools to deal with difficult situations.

ISAK (International Students at Kenyon): To promote cultural and ethnic education on campus through the talks given mostly by the international students themselves.

Multi-Cultural Council: The purpose of the MCC is to create a unified entity of campus cultural organizations, including: Black Student Union, Adelante, ASIA, Crozier Board, ALSO, Snowden Programming Board, AJASK, ISAK, Hillel, NIA, and Brothers United. MCC provides networking opportunities, educational programs, and political awareness for all campus organizations, faculty, staff, and administrators.

SCA (Students for a Creative Anachronism): "The SCA is an organization dedicated to researching and recreating the customs, combat, and courtesy of the Middle Ages. We build weapons, armor, and shields, and fight with them. We hold and attend tournaments and revels. Members study and practice armory, dance, calligraphy, embroidery, fencing and many other lost arts and sciences."

1033: Bring the funny.

Beyond Therapy: Sketch comedy group that writes their own material and performs one major show per semester.

Fools on the Hill: An improvisational comedy group

providing a theatrical outlet to the Kenyon community without cost or other requirements.

GREAT (Gambier Repertory Ensemble Actors Theatre): To provide funding and support for student run, student directed, and student produced theatrical endeavors.

KCBDC (Kenyon College Ballroom Dance Club): This club provides ballroom dance instruction from skilled students as well as a professional teacher. The club is not exclusive to any experience or interest level. Ballroom dance includes waltz, tango, foxtrot, cha-cha, rumba, swing, etc., as well as more social dances such as salsa, merengue, lindy hop and hustle. Dancers may travel with the club to intercollegiate competitions if interested. If you like to dance, that's literally all you need to join.

KCDT (Kenyon College Dance Team): To provide support for sports teams and entertainment for fans.

KMT (Kenyon Musical Theater): KMT provides an outlet for student produced musical theater at Kenyon. All students work in produc-

tion aspects of the musical, including acting, directing, choreographing, stage managing, and production, construction of sets, costumes, and scenery.

Stage Femmes: Student-run theater organization that seeks to provide the Kenyon community with a high-quality theater about women and women's issues.

The Company: The Company provides an outlet for student-produced musical theatre at Kenyon. We hope to give students the chance to direct, choreograph, and perform in a number of songs and scenes taken from an entire spectrum of musicals. Auditions are held in the fall.

55%: A publication of the Crozier Center Program Board.

Reveille: The college yearbook is published annually and is distributed to graduates early in the Fall Semester of the following year. Any student is welcome to participate, and it is an excellent opportunity to hone editing, photography, and layout skills. The many dedicated participants of the yearbook do their darnedest to publish a quality book.

HIKA: HIKA is Kenyon's oldest student-run literary journal, providing an excellent outlet for the poetry, prose, and artwork of Kenyon students and faculty each academic year. Staff members are involved in all aspects of the magazine, from the selection process to the final layout.

Horn Gallery Literary Magazine: The Horn Gallery Magazine offers an opportunity for every student to express, in writing, any opinion or belief they have; as long as it is thoughtfully or artistically expressed. In addition, we publish all kinds of political commentary, as well as a small amount of poetry and prose.

Kenyon Collegian: A student-run weekly newspaper focusing on events on campus and in the Gambier community. It includes a regular format of news, features, commentary, sports, arts and entertainment, photographs and original cartoon work.

KFS Kenyon Film Society: Is composed of and directed by students; KFS is responsible for selecting and projecting the films shown each weekend throughout the academic year. In addition, KFS sponsors projection and production of student-made films, and provides a forum for the discussion and criticism of the art form. Free to the Kenyon community.

KJAS (Kenyon Japanese Animation Society): Exists to bring together fans of Japanese Animation and to introduce the Kenyon community to animation as a viable medium for complex storytelling and artistic expression.

KSF (Kenyon Student Filmmakers): To create an opportunity for Kenyon students to write and direct films and videos. In addition, our services would be available for other college events and activities, as we hope to establish an annual Kenyon Film Festival.

Pierce Darkroom: Supplies darkroom access and materials to publications on campus, specifically the yearbook and newspaper.

Kenyon Visuals: Kenyon Visuals is a glossy, full color publication of artwork produced by art students.

Persimmons: Persimmons is an outlet for the very best creative efforts of Kenyon's student body. It is a publication that embraces student poetry, prose, art, photography, and music, allowing talented writers and artists to share their work with others.

The Kenyon Observer: TKO is a news magazine, which focuses on issues that affect the Kenyon community. TKO does not report news, it provides an opinion and criticism of trends and policies at Kenyon and in the country. TKO does have a conservative viewpoint, but welcomes all types of opinions and discourse, in order to help the community better understand important issues.

The Voice: The Kenyon Voice is a progressive political journal dedicated to inspiring creative rebellion. The Voice's aim is to provoke emotion and real physical response. The Voice isn't boring or reasonable. It doesn't understand negotiation. The Voice doesn't believe in statistics. It is provocative, irreverent and honest. And finally the Voice is serious about beliefs, and we all know beliefs are sexy.

WKCO: WKCO is an educational and entertainment medium for greater Gambier. WKCO offers the opportunity to participate in various facets of radio communication. Positions as interns, disc jockeys and executive staff members are available.

Greek Council: An agency of Campus Government that governs the fraternities and sororities. Duty is to coordinate the activities of its member groups, to promote a sense of purpose and community among the groups, and to draft legislation that affects all aspects of Greek Life.

Alpha Delta Pi: The principle purpose, as stated by founder Samuel Eells: That this association, with a true philosophical spirit, looking to the entire man, develop the whole being—moral, social, and intellectual.

Beta Theta Pi: The brothers of Beta Theta Pi take the idea of brotherhood seriously, becoming more diverse every year. Academics combined with extracurricular activities, enhance the Kenyon experience.

Brothers United: Kenyon's

most recent addition to Greek life is a fraternity established in 1994. The fraternity supports African and African-American males. It strives for excellence in all endeavors; community service is an integral part of the organization. The fraternity is open to all Kenyon men who possess certain academic criteria, and who show a genuine interest in the organization and its goals.

Delta Kappa Epsilon: The Lambda Chapter of Delta Kappa Epsilon, Kenyon's first fraternity, has graduated more US presidents than any other fraternity nationally, including Lambda's own Rutherford B. Hayes. The first fraternity lodge in America was also erected by the Lambda chapter.

Delta Phi: Seeks to promote the unilateral disarmament of anti-government militias in the hopes of their energy could be re-channeled into less violent pursuits. Also to limit the spread of Kudzu the scourge of our southeastern forests.

Delta Tau Delta: Originally, Delta Tau Delta was founded to correct an unjust campus situation. Since 1858 and its founding at Bethany College in what is now West Virginia, chapters have spread across the United States and Canada. Kenyon's Chi chapter, established in 1881, was one of the first Delt chapters in the nation. Members excel at community service, academic and athletic excellence, and leadership while maintaining a strong and social brotherhood.

Phi Kappa Sigma: The promotion of good fellowship and the cultivation of the social virtues among its members; the protection of the just rights and the advancement of the best interests, present and future, individual and collective, of all those who shall be associated together as members of the fraternity; the encouragement of good scholarship and breadth of training for its members; and cooperation in the educational and cultural programs of institutions of higher education in which chapters are located.

Psi Upsilon: Founded at Union College in 1833 and established its first chapter west of the Alleghenies at Kenyon in 1860. As President William Howard Taft, a member of Psi Upsilon, once said, "Psi Upsilon represents the character of men we need; men who are intellectual, who are strong, who are loyal, who have high ideals, have courage, have comradeship, and are for the public and the country all of the time without talking about it. The last is exceptional. I am glad and proud to belong to it."

Epsilon Delta Mu: sorority is based on the Greek philosophy of Eudemonia, the idea that a good life is based on friendship, happiness, knowledge, and virtue. Through these four ideas, we plan to enrich ourselves, our sisters, and the community as a whole.

NIA: To provide a service organization for the betterment of the African-American community at large and other minorities on campus. NIA promotes awareness of the achievements and needs of African Americans and other cultural and ethnic groups through planned events and projects. NIA serves as a support system through which sisterhood provides members with a common ground. With this system, we can help one another strive to achieve academic excellence. All women are welcome to join all functions.

Theta Delta Pi: To create a foundation of sisterhood through a support network, and to supplement academics with community service and social functions.

Zeta Alpha Pi: Through a core foundation of sisterhood, Zeta Alpha Pi advocates: the cultivation of the intellect and leadership; the fostering of positive relationships, individual and societal, through service to the College and the community; the embodiment of Kenyon College's values and beliefs, such as academic excellence; and the formation of interminable bonds, which enrich the college and post-college experience, and will be carried throughout our lifetimes.

Kenyon After Dark: The Mission of Kenyon After Dark (KAD) is to make available quality late night weekend entertainment between the hours of 9 p.m. and 2 a.m. The Kenyon After Dark Programming Board as well as other student clubs and organizations plan an array of events from game shows, to open mics, to bands and coffeehouses.

American Chemical Society:

The purpose of ACS is to promote chemistry education on campus, and in the community through our seminar series and public outreach programs.

Kenyon Debating Society: Competes in extemporaneous debate as part of the National Parliamentary Debate Association. Also competes in Model United Nations Conferences. Members develop their speaking and reasoning skills in practices, and put them into action at tournaments we travel to across the country.

Math Club: To promote mathematics and its awesome applications on campus.

Student Lectureships: It is the objective of the committee to enhance discussion, and stimulate thought about important issues in an entertaining and progressive manner. This committee of Student Council uses funding from Student Activity Fees to sponsor diverse, intelligent, and entertaining speakers for the Kenyon community.

Basement Music Club: The purpose of The Basement Music Club is to provide

individuals with information about the hip-hop/rap culture, to introduce people to the hip-hop/rap culture, and to provide a venue in which members of the hip-hop/rap culture can perform. Each member is to abide by all rules as given to him or her by the officers as long as it follows all college regulations.

Chasers: The Kenyon College Chasers, founded in 1964, is the oldest group of acappella singers on campus. This select ensemble of approximately fifteen men and women perform contemporary, original arrangements of songs by many different artists. Both on and off campus, the Chasers perform at college functions, musical revues, and community receptions. Each semester, a full-length concert, held in Rosse Hall, is performed. In January, the Chasers will tour for approximately seven to ten days. Open auditions will be held in early September.

Cornerstones: Since the spring of 1998, the Cornerstones have voiced the Christian message with a cappella and instrumental performances of spirituals, contemporary Christian, and secular styles of music. We perform one concert a semester, sing at various campus events, and about once a month at area churches.

Groove squad: Offering the best in motivational music at Kenyon football and basketball home games, the pep band is always looking for more talented instrumentalists.

Kenyon College Gospel Choir: To bring the tradition of Gospel music in American culture to the Kenyon campus and surrounding communities.

Kokosingers: The Kokes -- the oldest, all male a cappella singing group on campus -- holds auditions in early September. Sign up during the Activities Mart. The Kokes' repertoire ranges from traditional to contemporary arrangements. There are three concerts and a Fall and Winter tour. All are invited to audition regardless of previous a cappella experience.

Owl Creek Singers: The Owl Creek Singers is a student-run, a cappella vocal group of approximately ten women. These women of music and melody perform two concerts, a Revue, a ten day tour over break, and sing at College and local events. The group has an eclectic, ever-changing repertoire that ranges from soul and pop music to oldies. Auditions are held in the fall.

Pealers: The College Pealers serenade the campus with the chapel bells every Friday afternoon, on holidays, and during academic ceremonies such as Honors Day and Graduation. The Pealers perform traditional bell ringing, hymns, school songs, and the occasional pop tune as part of a long time Kenyon tradition.

Stairwells: Kenyon College's only folk group, made up of a variety of musicians and vocalists. What makes the Stairwells unique from the Kokosingers and the Owl Creeks is that we do both acappella songs and full band songs, so we welcome all musicians to try out, not just vocalists. The range of music covered in the past by the Stairwells has ranged from Paul Simon to G. Love, so there is no song that cannot be done. Rehearsals are at least three times a week for one hour, in which we rehearse for our two big concerts and all of our other shows in between.

Student Council: The Student Council, the official representative body for student discussion, organization, and action is composed of one representative from the three upper classes and the presidents of the sophomore, junior, and senior classes who are elected in the spring; one first-year representative elected in the fall; and the eight executive officers of the Council: the president, the vice presidents for student life and academic affairs, the chair of the Housing and Grounds Committee, the treasurer, the communications director, and the president of the First-Year Council. The student co-chair of Senate is an ex-officio member of Council. The chair of Student Lectureships, the chair of Social Board, and the chair of the Security and Safety Committee report to Student Council on a regular basis. The functions of the Council are to formulate and express officially student views concerning affairs of the College; to recognize legitimate student activities, enterprises, organizations, and social events and to supervise their operations; and to administer elections, appointments, and removals by impeachment for all student offices in the campus government.

First-Year Council: The First-Year Council is composed of an Executive Board—five building presidents, one of whom is the second representative to Student Council; one class representative to the Senate; and one class representative to Student Council—and five Residence Hall Committees—one representative from each hall/wing in each first-year residence hall. These groups meet on alternate weeks, with the Executive Board serving as the link between the two groups. The two main purposes of the Residence Hall Committees are: 1) to address building-specific issues and 2) to provide special events for the buildings. First-year students should approach either the president of their building or their specific hall representative with questions, comments, or suggestions.

Upper Class Committees: In the spring, the sophomore, junior, and senior classes elect a class president for the following year. The president of each class serves as a voting member of Student Council. A class committee of eight students, who work with the president to coordi-

nate class activities and promote class unity, is elected in
the fall. The class representa-
tives to Student Council and
Campus Senate also serve on
the class committee.

Activists United: comfort-
ing the afflicted, afflicting
the comfortable. Primarily
employing dialogue as a
vehicle for activism, we hold
discussions in order to incite
action among the Kenyon
community. Activities United
operates principally through
democratic process decid-
ing our own agenda i.e.
what issues matter to our
participants. We have focus
on direct action, not only
through the open confronta-
tion of important social issues
(via protests, rallies, etc.), but
also through volunteer work
within the local community.
Activists United will function
as a base of contact for all
activists on campus: inform-
ing them of political happenings locally, in addition to the
Midwest, the nation, and the
world.

Kenyon College Greens: Our
organization aims to start
a grassroots movement at
Kenyon College. We support
all local and national Green
Party candidates through
campaigning, information
drives, fundraisers, and voter

registration.

Kenyon College Republi-
cans: To educate our campus
about the Republican agenda
and to make the campus
generally more politically
aware and active.

Kenyon Democrats: To
organize the Democrats of
Kenyon to show the students
the views of the Democrat
party and encourage them to
get involved in politics.

SFT (Students for a free
Tibet): Educates and takes
action regarding human
rights violations in Tibet, the
Chinese Communist Party's
occupation of the formerly
independent Tibet, and
Tibetan culture.

Big Group Christian Fel-
lowship: To provide weekly
Christian fellowship for interested students.

Hillel: Hillel at Kenyon
College serves the Jew-
ish students, faculty and
staff by providing religious,
cultural, and social opportunities to explore, enhance
and celebrate their Jewish
heritage. Hillel also serves
the Jewish residents of Knox
County. Jewish students at

Kenyon College have the opportunity to take an active role in determining the shape of Jewish life on the campus by serving on the Hillel student programming board. Throughout the academic year, Hillel sponsors speakers, entertainers, has community dinners, organizes parties, film nights, trips to Columbus Jewish institutions for workshop, cultural and social events. Hillel regularly co-sponsors events with other Kenyon departments and organizations. In short, the goal at Kenyon College Hillel is to maximize opportunities for the Jewish population at and around the campus to explore Judaism and expand their knowledge of its traditions and culture through a wide variety of programs and events.

Newman Club: Newman Club is the umbrella group for Roman Catholic students at Kenyon. Members of the Catholic community in Gambier gather for mass each Saturday evening at 5:30 p.m. in the College Chapel. Students may serve as musicians, lectors, and Eucharistic ministers.

APSO (Appalachian People's Service Organization): The Appalachian People's Service Organization (APSO) does October and Spring Break trips to Appalachia, and a number of fundraisers and cultural/interpretive events throughout the year.

Circle K: World's largest collegiate service organization, and is designed to allow college students to play a more active, helpful role in the lives of community members and fellow students. Anyone with a willingness to serve, commitment to humankind, and dedication to the ideals of the organization are encouraged to join.

First Step: Student volunteers who lend a friendly ear and supportive conversation over the telephone to fellow students who want to talk. First Step is a resource for questions about Kenyon, from where classes are located to information about student groups. We also have information on many other topics, ranging from drug abuse to stress. First Step guarantees anonymity for callers—confidentiality is our guiding principle. The goal is to offer empathy, exploration of feeling and a discussion of alternative solutions. We are not counselors, we are peers—we are here to listen.

Habitat for Humanity: Works in collaboration with the Knox County Habitat chapter to build homes for low-income families. No skills necessary to participate.

OAPP (Off-Campus Activities in Psychology Program): A liaison between the students and various community agencies.

Kangeroos: To provide the town of Gambier with a volunteer child care option by creating a fun and educational learning environment.

KSA: Dedicated to promoting the general welfare of the student-athlete both at Kenyon and in the community at-large. KSA seeks to enrich the lives of student-athletes and promote them as positive role models through our projects at Kenyon and community service.

Snack Pak: We hope to implement social change by giving elementary school students the opportunity to have college-aged role models while also providing them with time for open social interaction with their peers, both of which have been proven to lower the amount of classroom disruption in elementary school students. In addition, we can help to build the bridges between the different communities in Knox County. Our aim is to work with West Elementary School in Mount Vernon, which is one of the lower-income schools in the county. We will go to the school one afternoon a week, provide a snack for the kids, and then either play games, read, or work on long-term projects, depending on the week.

Aids Committee: The AIDS Committee is committed to enhancing awareness about the HIV virus, providing protection against the virus, and educating the Kenyon community about the AIDS epidemic. We sponsor free, anonymous HIV testing twice a year, as well as provide condoms, dental dams, etc. for all students. Some past and future activities include speakers for World AIDS Day, The Names Project AIDS Quilt display, volunteering at an AIDS hospice, AIDS charity benefit concerts, and other various fund raisers.

Amnesty International: Works for the promotion and protection of human rights the world over. The Kenyon chapter of AI works towards this goal primarily through letter writing to international (and United States) government officials, and also through campus awareness-raising activities.

Archon Society: A coed community service and social organization, which provides a bridge between Kenyon students and residents of Knox County through volunteer activities. Upper-class new members are accepted in the fall and spring, while first-year students are accepted in the spring, coinciding with Greek Rush.

BFEC (Brown Family Environmental Center): To create opportunities for individual and collaborative study of organisms and habitats of Central Ohio, and to benefit the general public of Knox County through environmental education and recreation consistent with its educational goals.

Cooperative Bookstore: A Co-op bookstore is a valuable and vital part of any university. Kenyon's Co-op closed down as special interest housing last year. We propose to restart it as a club to achieve greater exposure

and success.

Kenyon Men Against Sexual Violence: Sexual assault is a serious problem across the country and on our campus. There are things that men can do to create a safer and more respectful environment. Our goal is to provide education and support for men so that the incidence of sexual assault is reduced.

Kenyon Zen Meditation Group: Everyone has a personal purpose for meditation; ranging from enlightenment to a study break.

Peeps O'Kenyon Guided by the ideology of purity and accuracy, we disbanded from national fraternal ties in 1970 to achieve greater creative independence and initiative with the Kenyon Community. In 1974, female members were accepted to form a more perfect aura within our state. We are balanced and continuous people, Torque Mortem Talpem Supra Tuum Caput Dum Vivimus Vivamus!

REEL (Resources and energy efficient living): To help Kenyon become a more environmentally responsible place. Our ultimate goal is to create an environmentally friendly, low-impact living situation for students on campus.

SMAC (Student Medical Advisory Council): To facilitate interaction and understanding between the student body and the health center. Also, SMAC promotes the awareness of health related issues and the services provided by the health center.

Social Board: As a standing board of Student Council, Social Board strives to provide nonalcoholic activities and social programs for the entire student body throughout the school year. Members are selected by a letter of intent, which are collected by the board in the beginning of the school year. Members' attendance and participation of the events and weekly meetings is mandatory. As a result, members gain experience in the planning and production of events for the entire campus.

Sound Technicians: Maintain and operate sound equipment available for rent to organizations.

Student Volunteer Fire Department: The mission of the College Township Fire Department is to provide the highest quality of fire protection, and emergency medical services to Kenyon College and the surrounding community (College Township and Monroe Township).

Take Back the Night: To raise awareness about rape and help support rape survivors.

The Rolla Dyer Society: Supports and educates students interested in the health profession as a career. Members have the opportunity to perform volunteer service in health related fields, and to actively educate the campus and community.

Women's Collective: We are an organization designed to meet the needs, and build a community of Kenyon women. Unlike a sorority, we are all inclusive and seek to promote empowerment and communication across different classes and social groups, through education and social programs requiring active participation. The goal of these interactions is to develop and facilitate a support network whereby women have a richer voice within the Kenyon Community.

Club Soccer: To have a casual gathering of soccer players

Cycling Club: The cycling club promotes the use and enjoyment of bicycles through group rides, and the campus-wide purple bike program. In addition, a racing team competes in collegiate and open races in the fall and the spring.

Equestrian Team: Recognized by the Intercollegiate Horse Show Association, and offers competition to riders of all levels of experience, regardless of financial situation, and promotes sportsmanship, team enthusiasm, and horsemanship. The team recognizes the need for organized, competitive sports, and offers horse showing as an athletic opportunity at Kenyon College.

Fencing Club: Provides experience for beginners and intermediates in two weapons: foil and epee. Students teach the club in loosely structured practice sessions. Equipment is provided and experience is not necessary. Competition is encouraged, but enjoyment and learning are most important.

Ice Hockey: We are a club team of about twenty people that plays between ten and fifteen games per year. The season goes from Thanksgiving to around April 20th. We are a coed team that is open to anyone interested in playing. A few practices are scheduled each semester, and the schools that we compete against are Dennison, Oberlin, Case Western Reserve, EKU, Wittenberg and Wooster. Please contact Timur Senguen (senguent@kenyon.edu) or visit http://www2.kenyon. edu/orgs/icehockey/welcome.htm for more information.

Kenyon Chess Club: Provides an opportunity for members of the Kenyon and Gambier community to meet on a regular basis to play chess, and to encourage participation in regional tournaments of the USCF. Members also provide instruction for novices, and those who wish to improve their present skills.

Kenyon College Boxing Association: To provide and opportunity for training in the sport of boxing.

The Best & The Worst

The **BEST** Things About Kenyon:

1. The people

2. The campus

3. Easy connection with professors

4. Getting a great education without getting it forced down your throat

5. The Isolation of the hill

6. Summer Send-off

7. Acappella Concerts in Rosse Hall

8. Fifty cent hot dogs at the village market

9. Everybody knowing your name

10. The library as the student union

The WORST Things About Kenyon:

1	Facilities
2	Being surrounded by cornfields
3	Parking
4	Language classes that meet nine times a week
5	The isolation of the hill
6	Paltry attendance at sporting events
7	Drinking as social center
8	The incestuous dating scene
9	All-nighters in Gund Commons
10	Graduating

Visiting KC

The Lowdown On...
Visiting KC

Hotel Information

- The Kenyon Inn, Wiggin Street, 32 rooms, A/C, dining room, 740-427-2202.

- The Gambier House (bed and breakfast), 107 East Wiggin Street, 6 rooms with private baths, no pets, no smoking, 740-427-2668.

- Accent House (bed and breakfast), 405 North Main Street, 3 guest rooms with private baths, A/C, no children under fourteen, no pets, no smoking, 740-392-6466.

- AmeriHost Inn, 150 Howard Street, 59 rooms, 2 suites, indoor pool, sauna, continental breakfast, lunch, dinner, banquet facilities, 800-480-8221, 740-392-6886.

- Chaney Manor (bed and breakfast), 7864 Newark Road, 2 guest rooms with baths, 740-392-2304.

- Curtis Inn on the Square, 12 Public Square, 70 units, 3 suites, A/C, dining room, 740-397-4334.

→

- Felicia's Guest House (bed and breakfast), 10996 Banning Road, 3 guest rooms with shared bath, 740-397-2279.

- Heritage House (bed and breakfast), 307 North Main Street, 4 guest rooms, 2 baths, 2 nonsmoking rooms, no pets, 740-392-9301.

- Holiday Inn Express, 11555 Upper Gilchrist Road, 70 rooms, A/C, 800-465-4329, 740-392-1900.

- The Home Place (bed and breakfast), 1322 Wooster Road, 5 guest rooms with shared baths, 740-393-2301.

- Locust Grove Ranch (bed and breakfast), 12480 Dunham Road, 3 guest rooms with baths, 740-392-6443.

- Mount Vernon House (bed and breakfast), 304 Martinsburg Road, 7 guest rooms with private baths, children welcome, no pets, 740-397-1914.

- Mount Vernon Inn, 601 West High Street (U.S. 36), 12 units, A/C, continental breakfast, 740-392-9881.

- Oak Hill Bed and Breakfast, 1300 Park Road, 3-bedroom guest house with kitchen and private bath, 1 guest suite with private bath, 740-397-1672.

- Russell Cooper House (bed and breakfast), 115 East Gambier Street, 6 guest rooms with private baths, A/C, no children under twelve, no pets, 740-397-8638.

- Super 8 Motel, 1000 Coshocton Avenue, 49 units, A/C, pool and health spa, nonsmoking rooms available, 800-800-8000, 740-397-8885.

Take a Campus Virtual Tour

http://www1.kenyon.edu/visitors/tour/

Campus Tours

Morning and afternoon interviews and tours are available Monday through Friday (mornings only on Saturdays) when the College is in session.

Overnight Visits

You may stay overnight (Sunday through Thursday nights), in a campus residence hall. Overnight visits can be especially helpful to your decision-making process.

Directions to Campus

From the north or northwest, take Interstate 75 South to Findlay and exit onto U.S. 23/Ohio 15 South. Take 23 South to Ohio 95 East in Marion. Follow 95 East to Ohio 13 South in Fredericktown. Take 13 South to Mount Vernon. Or take Interstate 71 South and exit onto 13 South at Mansfield. Follow 13 South to Mount Vernon.

From South Main Street in downtown Mount Vernon, take Ohio 229 East (East Gambier Street).

From the east or northeast, take Interstate 71 South and exit on Ohio 13 South at Mansfield. Follow 13 South to Mount Vernon. From South Main Street in downtown Mount Vernon, take Ohio 229 East (East Gambier Street). Or take Interstate 77 South and exit onto U.S. 62 West. Follow 62 to Millwood and exit on U.S. 36 West. Follow 36 to Ohio 308 and turn left (south) onto 308, which leads directly into Gambier.

From the east or southeast, take Interstate 70 West and exit onto Ohio 13 North at Newark. Follow 13 North to Mount Vernon. Or take Interstate 77 North to Interstate 70 West. Follow I-70 West and exit onto 13 North at Newark. Follow 13 to downtown Mount Vernon. From there, turn right (east) from Main Street onto Ohio 229 (Gambier Street) to Gambier.

From the west or southwest, take Interstate 71 North from Columbus and exit onto U.S. 36 East. Follow 36 East to Mount Vernon. From South Main Street in downtown Mount Vernon, take Ohio 229 East (East Gambier Street).

Words to Know

Academic Probation – A student can receive this if they fail to keep up with their school's academic minimums. Those who are unable to improve their grades after receiving this warning can possibly face dismissal.

Beer Pong / Beirut – A drinking game with numerous cups of beer arranged in a particular pattern on each side of a table. The goal is to get a ping pong ball into one of the opponent's cups by throwing the ball or hitting it with a paddle. If the ball lands in a cup, the opponent is required to drink the beer.

Bid – An invitation from a fraternity or sorority to pledge their specific house.

Blue-Light Phone – Brightly-colored phone posts with a blue light bulb on top. These phones exist for security purposes and are located at various outside locations around most campuses. If a student has an emergency or is feeling endangered, they can pick up one of these phones (free of charge) to connect with campus police or an escort service.

Campus Police – Policemen who are specifically assigned to a given institution. Campus police are not regular city officers; they are employed by the university in a full-time capacity.

Club Sports – A level of sports that falls somewhere between varsity and intramural. If a student is unable to commit to a varsity team but has a lot of passion for athletics, a club sport could be a better, less intense option. If a club sport still requires too much commitment, intramurals often involve no traveling and a lot less time.

Cocaine – An illegal drug. Also known as "coke" or "blow," cocaine often resembles a white crystalline or powdery substance. It is highly addictive and dangerous.

Common Application – An application that students can use to apply to multiple schools.

Course Registration – The time when a student selects what courses they would like for the upcoming quarter or semester. Prior to registration, it is best to have an idea of several back-up courses in case a particular class becomes full. If a course is full, a student can place themselves on the waitlist, although this still does not guarantee entry.

Division Athletics – Athletics range from Division I to Division III. Division IA is the most competitive, while Division III is considered to be the least competitive.

Dorm – Short for dormitory, a dorm is an on-campus housing facility. Dorms can provide a range of options from suite-style rooms to more communal options that include shared bathrooms. Most first-year students live in dorms. Some upperclassmen who wish to stay on campus also choose this option.

Early Action – A way to apply to a school and get an early acceptance response without a binding commitment. This is a system that is becoming less and less available.

Early Decision – An option that students should use only if they are positive that a place is their dream school. If a student applies to a school using the early decision option and is admitted, they are required and bound to attend that university. Admission rates are usually higher with early decision students because the school knows that a student is making them their first choice.

Ecstasy – An illegal drug. Also known as "E" or "X," ecstasy looks like a pill and most resembles an aspirin. Considered a party drug, ecstasy is very dangerous and can be deadly.

Ethernet – An extremely fast internet connection that is usually available in most university-owned residence halls. To use an Ethernet connection properly, a student will need a network card and cable for their computer.

Fake ID – A counterfeit identification card that contains false information. Most commonly, students get fake IDs and change their birthdates so that they appear to be older than 21 (of legal drinking age). Even though it is illegal, many college students have fake IDs in hopes of purchasing alcohol or getting into bars.

Frosh – Slang for "freshmen."

Hazing – Initiation rituals that must be completed for membership into some fraternities or sororities. Numerous universities have outlawed hazing due to its degrading or dangerous requirements.

Sports (IMs) – A popular, and usually free, student activity where students create teams and compete against other groups for fun. These sports vary in competitiveness and can include a range of activities—everything from billiards to water polo. IM sports are a great way to meet people with similar interests.

Keg – Officially called a half barrel, a keg contains roughly 200 12-ounce servings of beer and is often found at college parties.

LSD – An illegal drug. Also known as acid, this hallucinogenic drug most commonly resembles a tab of paper.

Marijuana – An illegal drug. Also known as weed or pot; besides alcohol, marijuana is one of the most commonly-found drugs on campuses across the country.

Major –The focal point of a student's college studies; a specific topic that is studied for a degree. Examples of majors include physics, English, history, computer science, economics, business, and music. Many students decide on a specific major before arriving on campus, while others are simply "undecided" and figure it out later. Those who are extremely interested in two areas can also choose to double major.

Meal Block – The equivalent of one meal. Students on a "meal plan" usually receive a fixed number of meals per week.

Each meal, or "block," can be redeemed at the school's dining facilities in place of cash. More often than not, if a student fails to use their weekly allotment of meal blocks, they will be forfeited.

Minor – An additional focal point in a student's education. Often serving as a compliment or addition to a student's main area of focus, a minor has fewer requirements and prerequisites to fulfill than a major. Minors are not required for graduation from most schools; however some students who want to further explore many different interests choose to have both a major and a minor.

Mushrooms – An illegal drug. Also known as "shrooms," this drug looks like regular mushrooms but are extremely hallucinogenic.

Off-Campus Housing – Housing from a particular landlord or rental group that is not affiliated with the university. Depending on the college, off-campus housing can range from extremely popular to non-existent. Those students who choose to live off campus are typically given more freedom, but they also have to deal with things such as possible subletting scenarios, furniture, and bills. In addition to these factors, rental prices and distance often affect a student's decision to move off campus.

Office Hours – Time that teachers set aside for students who have questions about the coursework. Office hours are a good place for students to go over any problems and to show interest in the subject material.

Pledging – The time after a student has gone through rush, received a bid, and has chosen a particular fraternity or sorority they would like to join. Pledging usually lasts anywhere from one to two semesters. Once the pledging period is complete and a particular student has done everything that is required to become a member, they are considered a brother or sister. If a fraternity or a sorority would decide to "haze" a group of students, these initiation rituals would take place during the pledging period.

Private Institution – A school that does not use taxpayers dollars to help subsidize education costs. Private schools typically cost more than public schools and are usually smaller.

Prof – Slang for "professor."

Public Institution – A school that uses taxpayers dollars to help subsidize education costs. Public schools are often a good value for in-state residents and tend to be larger than most private colleges.

Quarter System (sometimes referred to as the Trimester System) – A type of academic calendar system. In this setup, students take classes for three academic periods. The first quarter usually starts in late September or early October and concludes right before Christmas. The second quarter usually starts around early to mid–January and finishes up around March or April. The last quarter, or "third quarter," usually starts in late March or early April and finishes up in late May or Mid-June. The fourth quarter is summer. The major difference between the quarter system and semester system is that students take more courses but with less coverage.

RA (Resident Assistant) – A student leader who is assigned to a particular floor in a dormitory in order to help to the other students who live there. A RA's duties include ensuring student safety and providing guidance or assistance wherever possible.

Recitation – An extension of a specific course; a "review" session of sorts. Because some classes are so large, recitations offer a setting with fewer students where students can ask questions and get help from professors or TAs in a more personalized environment. As a result, it is common for most large lecture classes to be supplemented with recitations.

Rolling Admissions – A form of admissions. Most commonly found at public institutions, schools with this type of policy continue to accept students throughout the year until their class sizes are met. For example, some schools begin accepting students as early as December and will continue to do so until April or May.

Room and Board – This is typically the combined cost of a university-owned room and a meal plan.

Room Draw/Housing Lottery – A common way to pick on-campus room assignments for the following year. If a student decides to remain in university-owned housing, they are assigned a unique number that, along with seniority, is used to choose their new rooms for the next year.

Rush – The period in which students can meet the brothers and sisters of a particular chapter and find out if a given fraternity or sorority is right for them. Rushing a fraternity or a sorority is not a requirement at any school. The goal of rush is to give students who are serious about pledging a feel for what to expect.

Semester System – The most common type of academic calendar system at college campuses. This setup typically includes two semesters in a given school year. The "fall" semester starts around the end of August or early September and finishes right before winter vacation. The "spring" semester usually starts in mid-January and ends around late April or May.

Student Center/Rec Center/Student Union – A common area on campus that often contains study areas, recreation facilities, and eateries. This building is often a good place to meet up with fellow students and is most commonly used as a hangout. Depending on the school, the student center can have a huge role or a non-existent role in campus life.

Student ID – A university-issued photo ID that serves as a student's key to many different functions within an institution. Some schools require students to show these cards in order to get into dorms, libraries, cafeterias, and other facilities. In addition to storing meal plan information, in some cases, a student ID can actually work as a debit card and allow students to purchase things from bookstores or local shops.

Suite – A type of dorm room. Unlike other places that have communal bathrooms that are shared by the entire floor, a suite has a private bathroom. Suite-style dorm rooms can house anywhere from two to ten students.

TA (Teacher's Assistant) – An undergraduate or grad student who helps in some manner with a specific course. In some cases, a TA will teach a class, assist a professor, grade assignments, or conduct office hours.

Undergraduate – A student who is in the process of studying for their Bachelor (college) degree.

ABOUT THE AUTHORS:

Writing this book was a benevolent challenge for me, it required a lot of time that as a senior is something I have little of, and a lot of deep reflection about my school and why I love it. I have affection for Kenyon that is indescribable, and could not imagine being happier anywhere else. Of my school and this book I am very proud. A book on Kenyon essentially writes itself, but if it were not for the energy, creative talent and wit of Zack Rosen it would not have been possible. Thanks and much respect to Logan Winston, for his unwavering support and guidance. I give my deepest gratitude to my parents, my sister, and my teachers for getting me through Kenyon, and the history department at Kenyon for teaching me to think here. On a lighter note, I am compelled to give shout outs to those who have made my Kenyon experience: Upper Norton, LSWG, Pink Thunder and the RA staff.

JayHelmer@collegeprowler.com

-Jay Helmer '04

As an English major, I often question whether or not I will be able to work as a writer when I graduate college. Now that I have actually gotten myself published, I think that I am one step closer to realizing that dream. I have never before had my writing printed outside of school newspapers and YM magazine, and I am still reeling in disbelief at the fact that my name is going to be on the cover of a book. The most important decision I have made in my life was my decision to attend Kenyon, and I hope that my love for the school shows through. Happy college hunting,

ZackRosen@collegeprowler.com

-Zack Rosen '06

P.S.—Extra thanks to my friends and my family, who I hope know what they mean to me. I owe a special debt of gratitude to Jay Helmer for giving me this incredible opportunity and turning "lanky" into a term of affection.

Notes

Notes

....

....

....

....

....

....

....

....

....

....

....

....

....

Notes

....

....

....

....

....

....

....

....

....

....

....

....

....

....

Notes

....

....

....

....

....

....

....

....

....

....

....

....

....

Notes

....

....

....

....

....

....

....

....

....

....

....

....

....

Notes

....

....

....

....

....

....

....

....

....

....

....

....

....

Notes

Notes

....

....

....

....

....

....

....

....

....

....

....

....

....

Notes

Notes

....

....

....

....

....

....

....

....

....

....

....

....

....

Need More Help?

Do you have more questions about this school? Can't find a certain statistic? College Prowler is here to help. We are the best source of college information on the planet. We have a network of thousands of students who can get the latest information on any school to you ASAP. E-mail us at *info@collegeprowler.com* with your college-related questions. It's like having an older sibling show you the ropes!

Email Us Your College-Related Questions!

Check out **www.collegeprowler.com** for more details. 1.800.290.2682

Notes

....

....

....

....

....

....

....

....

....

....

....

....

....

Tell Us What Life Is Really Like At Your School!

Have you ever wanted to let people know what your school is really like? Now's your chance to help millions of high school students choose the right school.

Let your voice be heard and win cash and prizes!

Check out **www.collegeprowler.com** for more info!

Notes

....

....

....

....

....

....

....

....

....

....

....

....

....

Do You Have What It Takes To Get Admitted?

The College Prowler Road to College Counseling Program is here. An admissions officer will review your candidacy at the school of your choice and create a 12+ page personal admission plan. We rate your credentials with the same criteria used by school admissions committees. We assess your strengths and weaknesses and create a plan of action that makes a difference.

Check out **www.collegeprowler.com** or call 1.800.290.2682 for complete details.

Notes

....

....

....

....

....

....

....

....

....

....

....

....

....

Pros and Cons

Still can't figure out if this is the right school for you?
You've already read through this in-depth guide; why not
list the pros and cons? It will really help with narrowing down
your decision and determining whether or not
this school is right for you.

Pros	Cons

Notes

....
....
....
....
....
....
....
....
....
....
....
....
....

Notes

....

....

....

....

....

....

....

....

....

....

....

....

....

Notes

....

....

....

....

....

....

....

....

....

....

....

....

....

Do You Own A Website?

Would you like to be an affiliate of one of the fastest-growing companies in the publishing industry? Our web affiliates generate a significant income based on customers whom they refer to our website. Start making some cash now! Contact *sales@collegeprowler.com* for more information or call 1.800.290.2682

Apply now at **www.collegeprowler.com**

Notes

....

....

....

....

....

....

....

....

....

....

....

....

....

Notes

....
....
....
....
....
....
....
....
....
....
....
....
....

Write For Us!
Get Published! Voice Your Opinion.

Writing a College Prowler guidebook is both fun and rewarding; our open-ended format allows your own creativity free reign. Our writers have been featured in national newspapers and have seen their names in bookstores across the country. Now is your chance to break into the publishing industry with one of the country's fastest-growing publishers!

Apply now at **www.collegeprowler.com**

Contact *editor@collegeprowler.com* or
call 1.800.290.2682 for more details.

Notes